A NEW APPROACH TO THE COMMUNAL PROBLEM

A NEW APPROACH TO
THE COMMUNAL PROBLEM

BY

RADHA KUMUD MOOKERJI

GYAN

Published by

Gyan Publishing House
5, Ansari Road
Daryaganj, New Delhi-110002
Phone: 011-47034999, 9811692060
E-mail: books@gyanbooks.com

Distribution Network
gyanbooks.com
India, USA, Canada, UK, Australia

ISBN: 978-93-6433-225-5 (PB)
First Published, 1943

2nd Impression 2024

Printed at: Gyan Press, Delhi.

A NEW APPROACH TO THE COMMUNAL PROBLEM
Author: RADHA KUMUD MOOKERJI

A NEW APPROACH TO
THE COMMUNAL PROBLEM

BY

DR. RADHA KUMUD MOOKERJI
M A., PH D , P R S

INTRODUCTION

Undoubtedly the name of Radhakumud Mookerji,—one of our most brilliant writers—is quite familiar to those interested in the various aspects of Indian History, Civilization and Politics, for he has contributed several learned books on these subjects To mention a few, " A History of Indian Shipping " (1912), " Local Government in Ancient India ", " Harsha ", also " Asoka," and " Hindu Civilization " etc

Since the author's Preface gives the readers of this book an idea of its contents, I shall not expand on it except to say that some of Dr Mookerji's views are apt to be very, very controversial But he *has* suggested reasonable ways and means of meeting India's communal problem which seem excellent and worthy of serious consideration

However, though I do not feel the necessity of enlarging upon the work itself, I think some notes on this extraordinarily clever man will not be out of place at all

From childhood upwards, Radhakumud exhibited a keen brain which won him honours galore. From Matriculation onwards, he always won distinctions and many notable scholarships His record at Calcutta University is astonishing, for he won the Cobden medal in Economics, the Premchand Roychand Studentship for Rs 7,000 and the Mouat Gold Medal

Later, having completed his brilliant academic career, he was offered the post of Hemchandra Basu

Mallik Professor at National Council of Education, Bengal, of Manindra Professor at Benares Hindu University and of Professor of History at Mysore University. At present, he is the Head of the Department of History at the University of Lucknow.

Dr. Radhakumud Mookerji's interest in Politics is not merely theoretical. From 1938-1940 he was a Member of the Bengal Land Revenue Commission under Sir Francis Floud who was the Chairman. He was the Vice-President of the Hindu Mahasabha for several years and was President of the Panjab Youths' Conference in 1936. He had been for 6 years a member of the Bengal Legislative Council on the Congress ticket, and the Leader of its Opposition for some time.

Added to all these honours, he was recently awarded the title of *Itihasa Siromani* and the Sayajirao Gaekwar prize of Rs. 7,000 by the Government of Baroda.

Dr. Mookerji is vitally interested in Minority problems on which he has addressed many public meetings for years and has contributed several illuminating articles. Hence, we consider ourselves very fortunate in having secured this brilliant man to write for us on one of our pressing problems of the day.

PREFACE

The present work represents in an abridged form the results of my study of the Indian Communal Problem in all its aspects and bearings on which I have also spoken and written much all these years. My first essay on the subject was published in London as far back as 1914 under the title, 'The Fundamental Unity of India,' to which an appreciative Introduction was contributed by the late British Premier, Mr. J. Ramsay MacDonald. The Communal Problem has become more and more complicated through the years since it was given a statutory recognition by Lord Minto in 1907 in reply to the demand presented to him by a Deputation led by the Right Hon. the Aga Khan. That Deputation was described and condemned as a "command performance" by the late Maulana Mohammad Ali as President of the Indian National Congress. This allegation has been admitted in a Government Document, the Report of the Indian Central Committee of the Statutory Simon Commission in which (p. 117) it is stated "that there was no *spontaneous* demand by the Muslims at that time for separate electorates, but it was only put forward by them at the instigation of an official whose name is well-known." This fact only shows up the underlying principle of British Government to divide and rule India. It is, however, to be noted to the credit of Lord Minto that though he conceded communal separate electorate, he conceded it strictly as a Minority Right. Accordingly, the Minto-Morley Reforms did not grant Separate Electorate to the Muslims of the Panjab, as they were not a minority there Lord Morley preserved his reputation as a leader of the English Liberal Party by fastening on Lord Minto the discredited device of Communal Electorate which has no parallel or precedent in any democratic Constitution. In his *Recollections* (II 325) he writes to Lord Minto 'I won't follow you again into our Mahometan dispute Only I respectfully remind you once more that it was *your* early speech about their extra claims that first started the M hare A lurid light is thrown on this episode which was thus engineered to forge an obstacle to the growth of India s national unity by the following passage cited by Lady Minto in her Diary from a letter received by her from a high official I must send your Excellency a line to say a very big thing has happened today a work of statesmanship that will affect India and Indian History for many a long year It is nothing less than pulling back of 62 millions of people from joining ranks of the seditious opposition

It is regrettable that in spite of unanimous nationalist opposition to separate communal electorates and amounts of representation in the legislature it was left to Montagu and Chelmsford, who were so eloquent in their Report in condemning them in theory as a negation of nationalism and democracy, in practice to grant them with vengeance to all communities whether Minorities or Majorities instead of confining them only to Minorities

From Communal Electorate and Communal reservation of seats in separate blocks in the Legislature to the demand for Pakistan is an easy and natural development. The spirit of separatism once generated and recognised by the Constitution grows on what it feeds on, and is now expressing itself in a philosophy of its own, culminating in a demand for the dismemberment of the country and a territorial separation of its communities on the ground that they cannot compose their differences in any other way In this work, I have ventured to present several other ways by which communities can compose their differences without going to the length and resorting to the extreme remedy of splitting up the country into separate Communal States and Sovereignties, with liberty to set up their own Unions by separate schemes of confederation The modern trend in politics is towards larger and larger Unions and Federations and is entirely against the disintegration of the existing Unions The Constitution of USA and Canada are pointers in this direction, while the USSR, which formed itself by giving to its primary and original Units the right to secede, is now moving towards a greater consolidation and centralisation of its Federal Government

At the same time, the USSR has the worst of communal problems beating hollow their Indian counterparts in their complexity, variety, and magnitude, and has solved them, without disintegrating the parent State, in a manner which is completely appropriate and applicable for India This work brings together all the schemes which have solved the Communal and Minority problems within the framework of the parent State in the hope that it may be found useful in suggesting ways and means by which the integral unity of India as a federated whole can be maintained and strengthened by a spontaneous union of all her communities in a spirit of loyalty to the common motherland which they may unite to build up as a democracy whose might and majesty will have to be reckoned with by the Comity of Nations in world politics

I wish to state in conclusion that I have freely adapted some of my previous writings to the present work.

April 1943 RADHAKUMUD MOOKERJI
Lucknow University

A NEW APPROACH TO

THE COMMUNAL PROBLEM

The Communal Problem a Universal Problem. The Communal Problem or the Problem of Minorities is not the special problem of India, but a universal problem It is not particular to any age or clime. No State in the world has ever been a homogeneous social composition constituted of only one community. The process of history has not made possible the evolution or construction of any State as a completely linguistic, religious, racial, or social unity. It has been a physical impossibility that political and national frontiers should also coincide with racial, religious, and social frontiers Such coincidence is getting more and more impossible in these days of easy, free, and speedy intercourse and communication between different Nations and Peoples, and the expanding facilities for emigration, colonization and settlement Of late, the free movement of peoples has been subjected to restrictions by different countries and States exercising their sovereign power to control and determine their social composition But this policy affects the future.

A State is called after its Majority community: Examples. For the present, every State in the world has been bound to accommodate different elements and communities in its composition At the same time, every such State finds within itself one community which forms the major part of its population It will naturally take and be called after it That is why we have countries called Poland Turkey Germany or Ireland That is why in Asia—*among the neighbours* of India—we have numerous countries designated after their respective majority communities Afghanistan, Baluchistan Turkestan Turkmanistan Arabistan, Luristan Khuzistan Kohistan Kurdestan Kafiristan Seistan (Sakasthana) Shahfistan Faristan Ardistan or Usbegistan Tadjikistan Baltistan Waziristan and Dardistan That is why India has also been known as Hindustan All these neighbours of India pay a com pliment to her culture by attaching the suffix *stan* to their names The term *stan* is derived from Sanskrit *Sthana* The naming adopted by so many countries after the Sanskrit manner shows how they have been India s good neighbours and have been influenced by her culture and civilization

No State can exclude a Minority At the end of the last Great War an attempt was made at a re-shaping of Europe on the basis of self determination This policy produced States like the Republic of Poland or that of Czechoslovakia But even these new States could not be constructed out of one community Poland and Czechoslovakia had each to accommodate substantial German minorities forming about a fourth of their populations As a matter of fact there is hardly any country in the world which is as large as India and yet is so homogeneous in its composition being peopled so largely by only one community

Thus the main problem of politics is the reconcilia tion of different elements and communities to a com mon citizenship owned by nationals of the same State

The ideal may be to create a State as a completely homogeneous unit, linguistic, racial or religious But the ideal has not been a reality in history It is also not physically possible to create a State after it A State may be dismembered into fragments in pursuit of this ideal but every such fragment will still have to accommodate a number of Minority communities along with the community in the Majority in the new State. All such flying fragments will be followed by Minority problems running after them and will have no escape from them There is also an economic limit to the fragmentation and size of a State

A saner approach to a stable political order lies another way It is to own to the unavoidable existence of Minorities in every State and boldly face the problems arising from them These problems have been the eternal problems of politics and tackled by different States in different ways in different periods of history

Treatment of the Problem in the Past: It may be recalled that in the eighteenth and nineteenth century, the governing principle of politics was the balance of power upon which rested the political equilibrium of Europe and the World With the development of democracy and the quickening of political consciousness and sense of nationalism, it was soon found that the sources of conflict lay in a less and less degree in the external relations of the State, but were growing up in their own internal conditions in which they were inherent They did not lie on the surface but lay deeper in the very composition and constitution of a State and appeared more and more to lie beyond the scope and purview of any superficial international diplomacy

A stable political order must depend upon the stability of its component and constituent parts It cannot afford to keep a sore point in any State The fundamental problem of every State is to unite its different elements in a common loyalty to its integrity and independence Quislings cannot find a lodgement in a wholesome body politic

One of the chief causes of the last Great War was the Minority problem The present Great War also arose out of the Sudetan Germans and the German Minority in Poland A stable world order must rest on a universally accepted solution of the problems presented by different communities and nationalities found in every State along with its major population

The problem of Minorities however which came to the front in the last Great War had been a problem of European politics for a very long time, though it received a scientific and comprehensive treatment for the first time at the end of that war in the provisions embodied in that behalf in the Treaty of Versailles The first treaty which contained definite stipulations concerning Minorities was the Treaty of Paris of March 30 1856 which followed the Crimean War It laid down expressly the obligation that in any country a class of subjects should not be rcognized as inferior to other classes for either religious or racial reasons From that date the question of racial or religious Minorities received greater attention at the hands of the governments concerned It should be noted, however, that the question was not yet regularly treated by any State as a part of its administrative policy. It was only raised on certain important historic occasions such as that of the annexation of a part of one State to another, or that of the constitution of new States, or that of territorial reconstructions resulting from a war, or that which resulted from struggles on the part of certain States against the oppression of other States Examples of this were the Treaty of Berlin of 13th July 1878 which imposed religious toleration on newly created States and on autonomous principalities (like Bulgaria, Serbia and Roumania) as an indispensable condition to an international recognition of their existence, and the Treaty of Vienna of 31st May, 1815 between the Netherlands, Great Britain, Russia, Prussia and Austria regarding the reunion of Belgium with Holland

These treaties may be, distinguished from those following the Great War by the fact that while the former confined themselves to the protection of individuals considered separately, the latter granted protection to Minorities recognized as collective groups or organized units, though this conception is not yet universally admitted and accepted even in the League of Nations

Its Treatment by the League of Nations: The problems of Minorities forming a fertile source of political trouble were naturally considered in all their aspects, bearings, variety, and complications at the end of the last Great War by the Peace Conference which met in Paris under the leadership of President

Woodrow Wilson, and solutions of these problems were settled by the collective wisdom and statesmanship which that Conference had represented The aim of the Conference was to establish a stable world order on its only possible basis in the principle of self-determination It was not however found easy to apply this ideal in the actual conditions that had established themselves in Europe in the course of history It was not feasible to write on a clean slate Political evolution had inevitably proceeded on other lines As has been already stated it is difficult so to order that each race should constitute its own State or to prevent different races from coming together in the same State The world is yet to know a completely homogeneous State constituted by only one community Therefore it was found to be practical politics to attempt only an approximation to the ideal of self determination by means of a corollary and a comprehensive scheme whereby different elements cultures and communities could be brought together in a single State and reconcile to a common government in ties of a common loyalty and citizenship

Thus the basis of a stable world order has to reckon with the fundamental fact that one Community State like the City States of ancient Hellas is a historical political and physical impossibility It must take into account the other fact of history namely that every State must inevitably be made up of a number of communities among whom one will be in the majority and the other communities will be Minority Communities The stability of a State as already stated must depend upon the degree of loyalty felt by its different communities to its integrity and sovereignty The only scheme by which this spirit of loyalty may be produced in its different communities so as to make them feel as citizens and nationals of the same State, will be to give protection to the Minorities in regard to those interests which they consider to be vital and fundamental to their separate existence as Minorities, and, beyond this field of protection, to treat them as the equals of the Majority community so as to lead them to be merged in a common citizenship upon which the State is based

Minorities Guarantee Treaties: A worthy attempt was made at the end of the last Great War, which was fondly supposed to be the end of all wars, to formulate a comprehensive scheme of Minority protection in order to stabilize the foundations of the different States of Europe and the world in a new order which would remove the causes of conflict between different communities and nationalities placed together in a common State The scheme was given a legal value in the form of Minorities-Guarantee-Treaties as international stipulations which were binding on the different States-Members forming the League of Nations which at one time comprised as its members as many as 52 different States of the World

Though the bloody history through which the world is passing has made a mockery of the League of Nations and the ideals for which it was constituted, it cannot be denied that these ideals mark out the only path of progress for the different nations of the world towards a world federation, "the divine event towards which the whole creation moves ' however ' far off" it may be for the present It is "the consummation to be devoutly wished for"

It may be useful to recall the extent to which progress was made by the League of Nations towards the elimination of the sources of conflict, which were inherent in many of the States of Europe in their minority problems from each such State in a new world order As many as 16 sovereign States of Europe gave their consent and signature to the stipulations concerning Minorities viz. 1 Albania 2 Austria 3 Bulgaria 4 Estonia 5 Finland 6 Greece 7 Hungary, 8 Latvia, 9 Lithuania 10 Memel 11 Poland 12 Roumania 13 Serb-Croat-Slovene Kingdom 14 Upper Silesia 15 Czecho Slovakia and 16 Turkey

All conceivable differences between communities living under a common State may be brought under one or other of the three following categories (1) Language (2) Race and (3) Religion

Definition of a Minority Numerical Test But firstly there is a limit to the recognition of a Minority It should not be open to any group of citizens to declare one fine morning that it feels that it has vital differences with the rest of their fellow citizens and then to set itself up as a Minority to claim special treatment and protection At the end of the last Great War this point was considered and it was agreed that a Minority to claim special treatment must be numerically large enough to form as is stated in the Turkish Constitution ' a considerable proportion of the population" It was also agreed that this "considerable proportion" should ordinarily be not less than 20% of the total population of the State. This numerical definition of a Minority was due to the fact that for a Minority of a smaller size, special treatment was not economically and administratively feasible. It is impossible for an administration to take cognizance of miscroscopic Minorities It is not economically possible, for instance, to concede to a Minority its own school where its children may have their primary education in their mother-tongue but where the number of such children is too small to make the formation of a school financially possible.

This numerical criterion of a Minority requiring it to constitute an adequate percentage or proportion of the country's population has been suggested by some important practical considerations and also imposes upon it certain fundamental obligations A Minority must not be at liberty to distribute itself through a country in any manner it chooses if it has to claim recognition Any special treatment which it requires for the protection of its particular interests must be shown to be economically and administratively feasible It must so distribute itself through the different parts of a country that it can register everywhere the minimum degree of density indicated above Nowhere should it dwindle into thinness that is not recognisable

It must not be a Migrant Minority: Another feature of a Minority is that it must belong to the country permanently This rules out immigrants. Immigrants as a minority cannot claim protection because as was pointed out at a meeting of the League of Nations Assembly they entered the country of their own free will and by assuming the nationality of the country, undertook to conform to its internal legislation Distinction should be drawn between immigrants and original inhabitants who having been transferred by treaty from one nationality to another might constitute what was known as a minority As a matter of fact the Minorities problem became more pronounced and acute in Europe after the last Great War ended by the treaty of Versailles That treaty undertook European reconstruction along three main lines viz (1) by the creation of new States to be peopled by communities of the largest majority in obedience to the principle of self-determination as comparatively homogeneous States (2) by modifying the frontiers of certain States to give scope to self determination and (3) by transferring to certain countries populations previously belonging to other States *The inherent difficulty of the situation has since re-*ceived a most forceful illustration in the Sudetan Germans

It may be noted in this connection that provisions for the solution of Minority problems in all their variety and complications together with a recognition of the rights of Minorities originated from Articles 86 and 93 of the Treaty of Versailles which are the source of the Treaties of June 28 and September 10 1919 the first concluded between Poland and the principal Allied and Associated Powers and the second between those Powers and Czechoslovakia The other Treaties con cerning Minorities were signed by the Central and Eastern European States concerned in 1919 and 1920, and placed under the guarantee of the League of Nations in the same way as the first two Treaties In 1921, when Finland and Albania were admitted to the League of Nations, they signed declarations which included the provisions of the Minorities Treaties Lithuania in 1922 and Latvia and Estonia in 1923 undertook similar engagements before the Council of the League of Nations with regard to Minorities The protection of Turkish Minorities in Greece and of Greek Minorities in Turkey was assured by Articles 37-45 of the Treaty of Peace of Lausanne of July 24, 1923, and by the protocol of the same date signed between the principal Allied and Associated Powers and Greece

Protection Limited to Differences of Race, Religion and Language The central feature of a scheme of Minority protection is to define and establish its differences from the rest of the citizens of the country on the basis of unmistakable and admitted grounds The grounds of such differences can be only of three kinds (1) racial, (2) religious or (3) linguistic The theory of Minority protection is that such protection is not permissible for any artificial, temporary, or accidental aspects or features which a Minority may acquire, assume, or take on in its career It must take its stand upon its native inherent, and fundamental features, and not upon any poses and fashions of the hour It must stand for its historic and cultural characteristics which alone are worthy of all respect and recognition so as to enable it to make its progress along its own lines of evolution and make its own contribution to the general culture of mankind.

The situation was well put at a meeting of the League Council of 9th June 1928 "The health of an organism requires organic balance, i e, harmony between its various organs Nature seems to have taken the most minute precaution for safeguarding all these small organs in order that the organism as a whole may not suffer In the same way sociology proves the utility and the necessity of the existence of small peoples There can be no doubt that in this world variety is indispensable to the symmetry and harmony of all fine things"

Every stable political order must be based on the bed rock of justice in recognising that the racial, religious and linguistic differences of communities their cultural characteristics must be preserved and promoted instead of being obliterated in the interests not merely of the communities concerned but in the larger interests of universal culture and civilization

Linguistic Protection. Its Constitutional Provisions There can be no two opinions on the position that a community is entitled to the cultivation of its own language and mother tongue It is entitled to claim that its children should be taught in and through the medium of their mother tongue in the primary schools It may also claim the use of the script in which its language is written It is again a just claim that the State must establish Minority educational schools where it is economically feasible on the basis of the number seeking such education.

The international stipulations on these points of Minority protection in regard to the supreme subject of education have been thus framed:

"A Minority school shall be established on the application of a national supported by the persons legally responsible for the education of at least 40 children of a liguistic minority, provided these children are nationals of the State, and that they belong to the same school district, that they are of the age at which education is compulsory, and that their parents intend to send them to the said school

"If at least 40 of these children belong to the same denomination or religion, a Minority school of the denominational or religious character desired shall be established on application

"Should the establishment of a Minority school be inexpedient for special reasons, Minority classes should be formed (in the general public schools)

"The Minority schools shall receive a share, *proportionate to the number of their pupils*, of the funds allowed for the budgets of the school districts for the ordinary maintenance of elementary schools, apart from the general administration expenses and grants-in-aid"

The Turkish Constitution has the following provisions

"As regards public instruction, the Turkish government will grant in those towns and districts, where a considerable proportion of non-Moslem nationals are resident, adequate facilities for ensuring that in the primary schools, the instruction shall be given to the children of such Turkish nationals through the medium of their own language This provision will not prevent the Turkish government from making the teaching of the Turkish language obligatory in such schools

In towns and districts where there is a considerable proportion of Turkish nationals belonging to non Moslem Minorities these Minorities shall be assured an equitable share in the enjoyment and application of the sums which may be provided out of public funds under the State Municipal or other Budgets for educational religious or charitable purposes

Another international instrument contains the following significant provisions

The fact that Associations devote themselves to the interests of Minorities as regards their language culture religion ethnical character or social relations cannot constitute a reason for prohibiting those Associations hindering their activities or preventing them from acquiring legal status

Racial Protection Along with language the racial protection of a Minority is admitted on all hands as one of its fundamental rights Every community is entitled to the preservation and expression of its racial integrity and individuality as reflected in its particular manners customs and personal laws the laws of marriage or inheritance and these must be declared as its sole concern in which other communities should have no say

Religious Protection The religious protection of a community has been long established in every civilized State The problem of religious protection is not however confined to communities It is as much needed within a community by its different sects The larger a community the greater will be its internal differences in regard to religious views giving rise to different schools of doctrines and sects based on different religious prac tices calling for their protection Even in the days of the great King Harsha, the controversies between *Hinayana* and *Mahayana* acutely divided the Buddhist world so that the Emperor himself at times became a partisan. The Emperor Asoka, however, was a pioneer of religious toleration, as he was the pioneer of Universal Peace based on non-violence In one of his famous edicts, Asoka lays down as the basis of religious toleration the preliminary recognition of the fundamental fact that there is an essence (*sara*) in every religion as the central truth round which accumulate its external features, its forms and ceremonies, which are no part of its essence, and that all religions have in common this essence upon which must be built up the common religion of mankind An attitude of religious toleration starting from this fundamental fact of the unity of all religions in their essential doctrines is to be cultivated on the basis of the following virtues, *viz* (1) restraint of speech or thoughtless criticisms (*Vacha-Gupti*) (2) a comparative study of different religions by which one may become a *Bahusruta*, and (3) meetings of the exponents of different religions at Parliaments of Religions in which they should participate in a spirit of concord (*Samavaya*) These principles which Asoka laid down about 2000 years back hold good even for today. Asoka's system was the precursor of Akbar's *Din-i-Ilahi*.

Its Constitutional Provisions Sometimes, the problem of religious protection defies solution on the basis of mere theory or ideal In such cases, its solution may follow the lines laid down in the Turkish Constitution in accordance with international settlement.

"All inhabitants of Turkey shall be entitled to the free exercise whether in public, or in private of any creed religion or belief the observance of which shall not be incompatible with public order and good morals

Turkish nationals belonging to non Moslem Minorities shall enjoy the same treatment and security in law and in fact as other Turkish nationals

In particular they shall have an equal right to establish manage and control at their own expense any charitable religious and social institutions any schools and other establishments for instruction and education with the right to use their own language and to exercise their own religion therein

The Turkish Government undertakes to take as regards non Moslem Minorities in so far as concerns their family law or personal status measures permitting the settlement of these questions in accordance with the customs of those Minorities

We may also invoke the Turkish Constitution in regard to the place of Minorities in Administration

Differences of religion creed or confession shall not prejudice any Turkish national in matters relating to the enjoyment of civil or political rights, as for instance admission to public employments functions and honours or the exercise of professions and industries

Turkish nationals belonging to non Moslem Minorities shall enjoy the same civil ond political rights as Moslems

All the inhabitants of Turkey without distinction of religion shall be equal before the law

All nationals shall be treated on a footing of equality as regards admission to public employments functions and honours, including military ranks and to public establishments and as regards the granting of degrees distinctions etc"

Removal of Civil Disabilities: Thus the idea of this scheme of Minority protection is to make the Minority cease to feel itself as a Minority by assuring to it the same part and place in the State as the Majority on the basis of a common citizenship. It will appear that the scheme has two aspects, negative and positive The negative aspect comprises provisions aiming at the abolition of all disabilities under which a Minority is likely to labour on the ground of differences of Race, Language, and Religion. By abolishing all these civil disabilities, the Minority is placed on a footing of equality with the Majority so as to enjoy all civil and political rights in common with the Majority Indeed, the rights of citizenship must be regarded as the common property of all the nationals of a State, irrespective of their differences The established international principle must be that all must be equal before law, and that "there shall be but one nationality in the State in the sense that all communities living in the same country are, politically speaking, the nationals of a common State."

Cultural Autonomy of Communities: There is, however, a positive aspect of this scheme of Minority protection. Besides removing the disabilities of the Minorities so as to make them the equals of the Majority on the basis of a common citizenship, the scheme offers positive protection to the Minorities in certain matters and interests which they consider to be vital to their self-expression. In the treatment of such matters and interests, the Minorities are given complete autonomy and independence. These matters and interests constitute the foundation of their separation from the Majority as communities which stand by themselves It should be agreed that in regard to these the Minority should not be placed under the rule of the Majority who should have no say in matters which concern it so vitally These are the supreme cultural interests of the community which it must be allowed to preserve and to promote, and that if needed out of the general funds of the State of which its members are nationals. These interests as explained above concern its language religion, and its race or the social system expressive of its racial individuality which it cannot be called upon to sacrifice at the altar of democracy or the rule of the Majority The *Cultural Autonomy of Communities* must be the necessary and agreed limitation upon democracy Democracy must provide for freedom of thought Political freedom must yield to spiritual freedom

Such a comprehensive scheme of cultural autonomy within the prescribed field leaves a large ground for co operation among the different communities who live together under a common State as its nationals It is only on the basis of such a synthetic scheme that a unitary State can accommodate within its fold different elements peoples and races bound together by ties of a common citizenship The unitary State should not function as a narrow and close corporation but must expand itself into a comprehensive cultural federation operating within its political framework Such a reconstruction of the Unitary

State will not leave any pretext or excuse to a Minority to secede from it, because, by its very scheme, and its provision of adequate constitutional safeguards, it anticipates and answers effectively in terms of law and statute all conceivable pretexts and demands for such secession.

Restriction of Majority Rule: The arrangement is that in certain defined spheres concerning the vital interests of a Minority, the ruthless rule of the Majority must not operate. The Majority must bow to the Minority in such spheres where it must have no say Thus the scheme provides for the fullest and most liberal protection to a Minority in a democracy which is otherwise based upon the rule of the elected Majority.

Limits to Minority Protection. Only it must be remembered that there is a limit to such protection The limit is the integrity of the State which all its communities must be equally concerned to defend at all costs, and which no community can be allowed to weaken in pursuit of exaggerated and extravagant ideas of protection tending towards disintegration of the State itself. The position has been very well explained in the statements issued from time to time at the meetings of the Assembly and the Council of the League of Nations by representative political leaders of the different States of the world

Maintenance of the Integrity of the Present State: The following citations will be appropriate on the subject

"It was certainly not the intention of those who had devised this system of Minorities protection to establish in the midst of a nation a community which would remain permanently estranged from national life The object of the 'Minority' Treaties was to secure for the Minorities the measure of protection and justice which would gradually prepare them to be merged in the national community to which they belong (Sir Austen Chamberlain)

It seems to me obvious that those who conceived this system of protection (of Minorities) did not dream of creating within certain States a group of inhabitants who would regard themselves as permanently foreign to the general organization of the country (M de Mello Franco)

We must avoid creating a State within a State We must prevent the Minority from transforming itself into a privileged caste and taking definite form as a foreign group instead of being fused in the society in which it lives If we take the exaggerated conception of the autonomy of Minorities to the last extreme these Minorities will become a disruptive element in the State and a cause of national disorganisation (M Blociszewski)

A perusal of the Treaties showed that the Minorities concerned were racial linguistic and religious minorities The authors of the Treaties had not intended to create groups of citizens who would collectively enjoy special rights and privileges they had intended to establish equality of treatment between all nationals of a State If privileges were granted to the Minority in any country inequality would be created between this Minority and the Majority this latter would be oppressed by the Minority and it would then be the Majorities Question which would have to engage the attention of the League of Nations" (M. Dendramis)

Feeling for the Fatherland It is however, to be understood that all these schemes for the protection of Minorities and safeguarding their special communal interests so as to reconcile them to a common and equal citizenship to be enjoyed with other groups of citizens under the same State depend for their success ultimately upon what can be called the psychological and spiritual factor The stability of a political system or a State does not depend so much upon law and statute as upon the degree of loyalty it can spontaneously evoke and command in its various groups of citizens or nationals to its integrity, individuality, and independence The conception of sovereignty assumes habitual obedience on the part of its subjects to its authority Such obedience should not have to be enforced That will detract from the efficiency of its sovereignty Similarly, the country as a whole, the preservation of its unity, must always be felt by all its citizens as their sole and supreme concern Such a feeling of patriotism or love of the country as a sacred, indivisible, and inviolable unity cannot be produced by parliamentary legislation When citizens forget their sense of differences in an overmastering love of a common motherland, the stability of its political system is assured The moral or spiritual factor counts for it more than any other factor, religious, economic, or military Patriotism or nationalism is not the artificial creation of any law or statute It must be a natural growth It cannot grow in the air but must have its roots in the Mother Earth It can only grow round a country as its centre Just as the soul of an individual unfolds and expresses itself in and through a physical vehicle, *vahana*, or the body, the soul of a people also must embody itself in a country which it can claim as its own and exclusive possession, and the means of its self-expression A Nation, like the Individual, rests on a physical basis by means of which it manifests and asserts itself as a real existence and factor in the political world. The primary requisite for the birth and growth of a Nation is the certainty fixity and permanence of its place in the sun and when that is secured, the other formative forces of nationality will emerge and come into play in due course "A common fatherland is preliminary to all national development round that living nucleus will naturally gather all those feelings associations traditions and other elements which go to make up a people s language and literature culture and religion and thereby establish its separate existence and individuality demanding its preservation and independent development as a cultural unit of value to humanity The unifying influence of a common country of common natural surroundings of common economic conditions is irresistible and will prevail against all disintegrating and dividing factors such as differences in manners and customs language and religion

Need of a National Home History does not testify to nomadic peoples making much progress in civilization until they rid themselves of their migratory habits and become a settled people bound to a fixed habitation

The Hindu s Conception and Worship of the Mother Country At first India meant only the land of the Sindhu which Darius I the powerful Achaemenian emperor spelt as *Hindu* in his Bahistun inscription of 516 B C and the Ionian Greeks (*Yavanas*) took as *Indos* Thus arose the terms *India* and *Hindu* in history to indicate a country and its people without any reference to its religion In course of time, the India of the Indus or Sindhu began to extend and to expand in the freedom of its geographical boundaries right up to the seas in different stages and ever-widening circles designated by their different names in the Sanskrit works of different ages In the *Rigveda*, in its Nadi-stuti (X 15), Mother India is worshipped and visualized no longer as the land of the Sindhu as it appeared to the Persians but as a much larger expanse of territory watered by several rivers enumerated from east to west, such as Ganga, Yamuna, Sarasvati, Sutadri (Sutlej), Parushni, (Iravati, Ravi), Marutvridha, Asikni (Chenab), Vitasta (Jhelum), Arjikiya and Sushoma The nucleus of the holy land called Brahmavarta, which lay between the Sarasvati and the Drishadvati and was the home of Rigvedic learning and culture at its best, expanded in the course of history into Brahmarshi-desa comprising Kurukshetra and the country of the Matsyas, Panchalas, and Surasenakas (Manu, II 19), and this again into Madhyadesa (between Himalayas in the north, the Vindhyas in the south, Prayaga in the east, and Vinasana in the west) ; and further into Aryavarta [lying between these two mountains, and extending as far as the eastern and western oceans (Manu, XXI-22, 'that land where the black antelope naturally roams']. At the same time, the Vedic political ideal as expressed in the *Aitareya Brahmana* VIII, 20) was the extension of the country 'up to its limits in the ocean' under the dominion of a 'sole, single sovereign' aptly called *Ekarat* Thus ultimately the whole of the Indian continent from the Himalayas to the sea came to be assimilated by the Hindus as their indivisible mother-country to which was applied the new appellation, *Bharatavarsha*. The *Puranas* understand by the term *Bharatavarsha* "the country that lies north of the ocean and south of the snowy mountains." The leaders of thought in ancient India now addressed themselves assiduously to the supreme and sacred task of spreading among the masses and millions of India a living sense and conception of what constituted their mother-country as the object of their national worship. The founders of her religious systems were busy formulating national prayers by which Mother India was to be visualized and contemplated in worship.

Prayers for Worship of Mother India: The contribution of the Hindu to political thought is this deification of the motherland. The mother country is adored as the great Mother of all mothers. The national Sanskrit utterance is *Janani Janmabhumischa Svargadapi gariyasi*, 'the Mother and the Motherland are greater than Heaven itself.' The worship of the country is made a part of religion. Patriotism or nationalism is elevated into a religion.

Hindu sacred texts define the physical and visible form in which this new deity of Mother India is to be envisaged in meditation. They present the *Viratdeha* of Mother India as comprehending the entire continent stretching from Kashmir to the Cape. This will be evident from certain significant prayers which are to be uttered in common by all Hindus, irrespective of their different sects or creeds. They give expression to a common national sentiment centering round the Mother country. In one prayer, the country is called and invoked as the land of seven sacred rivers, Ganga, Yamuna, Godavari, Sarasvati, Narbada, Sindhu, and Kaveri, 'the commingling of whose holy waters is contemplated to impart its collective purity to the purificatory bath prescribed before worship." But the immediate effect of the prayer is that the Madrasi who utters it on the banks of the Kaveri feels a bond of union with the Indian of the north-west who bathes in the sacred waters of the distant Sindhu with the same prayers on his lips as worshipper of the same national deity.

Another prayer represents a different angle of vision from which the country is to be contemplated. The country is described as the land of seven sacred mountains forming as it were its ribs and backbone. These are Mahendra, Malaya, Sahya, Riksha, (mountains of Gondwana), Vindhya and Paripatra (western Vindhyas up to the Aravallis).

There is a third prayer offered to the country known for its seven sacred cities: Ayodhya, Mathura, Maya (Hardwar), Kasi, Kanchi (Conjeeveram), Avanti and Dvaravati (Dwaraka), the givers of salvation (Mokshadayika). The Hindus are enjoined by this prayer to visit these holy places by visiting which they have practically to go over the whole of India and think of it as their common sacred motherland.

Pilgrimage as Mass-Education in Nationalism: Sankaracharya, the great philosopher, purposely planted his four principal *Mathas* at the four cardinal points of the Indian continent: Joshi Matha in Badri-

Kedara up in the north, Govardhana Matha at Puri at the eastern most point Sarada Matha at Dwarka in the extreme west and the Sringeri Matha in the far south, so that by visiting these the pilgrim will know every inch of the sacred soil of his vast Mother Country

In fact Hindu sacred literature has covered the whole of India with a net work of holy places connected with one or other of the three principal Hindu deities, Vishnu Siva and Sakti The worship of Sakti is located at fifty two *Pithasthanas* or centres of pilgrimage distributed throughout the country Innumerable are the sacred places dedicated to the worship of Siva and Vishnu It was left to our immortal poet Rabindra Nath Tagore to give expression to this immemorial religious tradition in his inimitable song representing the *Virat Deha* the great body, of Mother India as having her sacred feet washed by the deep blue ocean in the south her forehead formed by the Himalayas her crown by their perpetual snows while out of her breats flow the streams of ambrosia in the great rivers, Jahnavi and Yamuna

Vision of India as a Federated Whole through the Ages It would appear that this religious conception of the mother country as a sacred entity has no place for its secular divisions into the so-called Provinces and States Religion has no place for such divisions which only operate on the material plane Spirit conquers Matter That is why Dwarka in the State of Baroda is as dear and sacred to the Hindus of all parts of India as is Puri in the British India Province of Orissa or

Benares in U.P The continental sacredness of Amarnath in Kashmir vies with that of Ramesvaram at the southern most point of the Madras Presidency. Every Hindu will flock from all parts of India to Gaya as the place marked out for the worship of ancestors Religion makes short work of all barriers, geographical, social, political, or communal Loyalty to India as a whole transcends all local or sectional loyalties as the supreme religion Thus the Hindu has given to citizenship a most stable basis in religion and spirituality The federation of the whole of India which is politically divided into so many States and Provinces has been an accomplished fact of Indian thought through the ages The indisputable geographical unity of India which is isolated from the rest of the world by its unmistakable boundaries and undisputed frontiers has been transformed by its history into a distinct cultural unity. The country becomes a spiritual entity because the spiritual enters more into its conception than the material The country is adored because it is the embodied type of a living culture Indeed, one may say that the culture is one's country and the country one's culture "The soul moulds the body as the body expresses the soul, but the genius of the nation is a vast presence which transcends its actual physical or geographical embodiment, and in its ideal possibilities can indeed embrace the whole world of man. Thus the evolution of India as the mother country of the Indians has but followed the lines of the cosmic process revealing the Universal in the Particular and the Particular in the Universal Here is no insular culture lacking in universality, nor a disembodied one which is homeless and therefore infructuous and sterile '

The idea was very well expressed by the late British Premier, J Ramsay MacDonald in his Introduction to my work The Fundamental Unity of India ' which was published as far back as 1914 The Hindu, from his traditions and his religion regards India not only as a political unit naturally the subject of one sovereignty—whoever holds that sovereignty, whether British Mahomedan or Hindu—but as the outward embodiment as the temple—nay, even as the goddess mother—of his spiritual culture

India and Hinduism are organically related as body and soul."

The Country as a Spiritual Entity Accessible to all

This initial Hindu conception of the country has inevitably had its own effects on its history Where the country counts more for its culture than as a material possession it appeals less to the instinct of appropriation There is more of disinterested sharing more of community of life and enjoyment There is a difference in political values Stress is laid on an extra territorial nationalism on the ideal of a larger citizenship in the kingdom of the spirit on a catholic and cosmopolitan outlook. India thus early became the happy home of many races cults and cultures flourishing in concord without seeking supremacy through mutual strife and extermination. India thus became the land of composite systems in respect of race language civil and personal law social structure and religious cult

India's Synthesising Social System: Indeed, there cannot but be differences of thought and belief, of manners and customs, among a people forming a sixth of mankind But Hinduism through the ages has stood for a principle of comprehension and synthesis by which all such differences may be reconciled as parts of a common complex It does not believe in a uniformity of thought and faith. The result is that Hinduism to-day by a process of assimilation of different elements through the ages is the most composite, complex, and comprehensive culture-system of the world giving accommodation within its all-embracing fold to peoples in all stages of social evolution from the lowest to the highest Hinduism has solved the problem of colour more satisfactorily than the U.S.A its Negro problem, or the South African Union its Indian problem While these countries solve their problems by ignoring them and by a simple policy of separation and segregation, Hinduism solves its problem by its principle of assimilation. It has treated the vast aboriginal peoples of India numbering more than 30 millions not by a negative policy of letting them alone, of segregating them, and avoiding contact with them. On the contrary, as a consequence of intimate and fruitful contacts, these primitive peoples have been dragged out of their isolation, their haunts in hills, and fastnesses of forests, to tread the paths of civilization opened up to them and have been subjected to a process of assimilation to Hindu society Most of these peoples have now become Hinduised, adopting for their worship Hindu gods and goddesses, priesthood for their social life and Hindu rituals ceremonies, and festivals like Holi and Devali Some of these like the Hos follow abstract Hinduism by calling their religion *Satya* or *Punya Dharma* taught by Gurus by worshipping one God by *Dhyana, Japa* or regulated meditation wearing sacred thread, bathing daily abjuring dancing and drinking and even giving up worship of idols or minor deities

Hinduism by its comprehension and synthesis is thus one of the most potent forces for building up a nation out of the most divergent elements

India's Social Homogeneity India is thus very well prepared by her history and traditions for a reconcilia tion of the different elements entering into the social composition of the State on the basis of a comprehen sive scheme of citizenship Her own social composition favours the evolution of a synthetic unity Out of her vast population of 380 millions as many as 300 millions belong to one religion This fundamental factor imparts to India a degree of social homogeneity which is rarely seen in any other country or State in the world

A Territorial Separation of Communities is no Solution of their Differences and Problems Possess ed of these spiritual social and historical factors India should have the least difficulty in settling her communal problems But as a matter of fact these problems are getting more and more complicated and remote from settlement till the extreme cry is raised that the only solution of these problems lies in the revolutionary and drastic step of a territorial sepa ration of communities, even at the cost of disintegrating the parent State, and splitting it up into fragments on the pretext of self-determination This is solving communal problems with vengeance by wiping out the very existence of communities This is utter defeatism, a confession of complete failure to bind different communities in ties of loyalty and equal citizenship to a common State If a community finds itself in a majority in a particular province, that should not be a ground for setting up such a province as a separate State by itself as the homeland of that community Such a claim is logically answered by the preliminary position that India as a whole has been the historic homeland of a particular community forming 75 per cent. of its total population 'As has been pointed out above, a mere territorial separation of communities cannot end the communal problem. It is not possible for communities to separate so that each may find and found a State by itself, from which other communities may be excluded There is no State or country in the world which is formed of one community A saner approach to the problem lies in the scheme of the Cultural Autonomy of Communities, the objective being to preserve the integrity of the country or the parent State at any cost, as is done in the two largest democracies of the world, the USA and the USSR

Right of Secession in the USA: The USA went to war on the issue of the right of the part of a State to secede from it On the eve of the American Civil War, Abraham Lincoln made his historic declaration· "I hold that the Union of these States is perpetual No State upon its own mere action, can lawfully get out of the Union"

The Communal Problem of USSR Perhaps the Russian example is more to the point for India The USSR is carrying on with communal problems at their worst It has to deal with the largest number of communities presenting the most profound and the widest possible differences linguistic racial or religious A history of its treatment of communal problems of such colossal complexity and magnitude is fraught with great significance for the treatment of communal problems in India where the differences between communities are far less fundamental and radical than those of USSR

Social Composition of USSR We may begin by drawing a picture of the social composition of the Union of Socialist Soviet Republics The Union comprises (1) a population of 170 000 000 (2) 180 different nationalities (3) 151 different languages (4) 11 National Republics and (5) 22 Autonomous Republics A Constitution that can bring together under one government such a huge number of different elements is a unique political achievement Besides the Russian communal problem as it was bequeathed to the Soviet Union by the Tsarist regime was bristling with difficulties of the first magnitude To understand this fully we have to go closely into the social organisation of the Union

Its Eleven Constituent Union Republics The eleven national Republics as they are called consist of (1) Ukraine (2) White Russia (Byslorussia)

(3) Georgia (4) Armenia (5) Azerbaidjan (6) Kazakhs (7) Kirghiz (8) Uzbeks (9) Turkmens (10) Tadjiks and (11) the RSFSR, where the Great Russians predominate, numbering about 116 millions, Ukraine has a population of about 33 millions, White Russia, over 5 millions; Transcaucasia, over 7 millions, Uzbekistan, about 5 millions; Turkministan, over 1 million, and Tadjikistan, over 1 million.

Its Twenty-two Autonomous Republics. The second category of national territorial formations comprises what are known as the Autonomous Republics These are constituted by territories belonging to one or the other of what are known as National or Union Republics, but peopled by minorities of different nationalities These Autonomous Republics are thus distributed; Sixteen on the territory of the RSFSR, one in that of the Ukraine, two in that of Georgia, one in that of Azerbaidjan, and one in that of the Uzbeks.

Their Heterogeneous Composition: Some of the regions thus defined are also heterogeneous in their social composition In Crimea, there live the Moslem Tartars. The region of the Caucasus is a medley of races and cultures In the North, the Russians, chiefly Cossacks, form the majority, while Transcaucasia is the happy home of a number of peoples like the Georgians, the Christian Armenians, and the Azerbaidjan Turks, each numbering between one and three millions. To the north-east of the Caucasus, on the grasslands bounded by the lower Volga, are settled the Kalmucks who are Mongols by race and Buddhists by religion East of the Volga, the steppe merges into the vast wastes and pastures of Turkistan divided between the two sections of the Turkish race known as Kirghiz and the Kazakhs each numbering between three and five millions Further east, in Central Asia to the south of these prairies live about five million Uzbeks, one million Turkomans and between one and three million Tadjiks The same medley of races is to be found in Siberia. Its western part is predominantly Russian, with a sprinkling of aboriginal tribes who live by hunting and fishing The Russians are also numerically strong in the Amour region of the far east and also in the maritime areas of the Pacific Eastern Siberia is divided between the Yakuts a Turkish race, and by the Burgats who are Mongolians

Besides these important nationalities, there is a number of smaller groups with considerable populations such as the Tatars of the Volga and the Crimea numbering about a million, the Jews who are settled mainly in the Ukraine and White Russia and number four millions the Germans and Finns of the Volga each numbering a million, and the Tchuvash of the Nizhni Novgorod region also numbering over a million

This is in short the ethnic map of the Soviet Union and a picture of its heterogeneous social composition

Policy of Tsarist Regime to Divide and Rule It is to be noted that the Tsarist regime was *not* interested in the unification of these various peoples in any well thought out synthetic system On the contrary, it preferred them living on terms of great hostility with one another In Transcaucasia for example the Azerbaidjan Turks and the Armenians were constantly at strife with each other, resulting in periodical massacres of large populations. In Georgia, the landlords and merchants, who were Armenians, were dearly hated by the people at large. In Central Asia, the Uzbeks as the dominant people were always having bloody feuds with the Turkomans These Uzbeks were not also on friendly terms with their neighbours, the Tadjiks Sometimes, the conflict of races was due to differences of religion, as in the cases of Shia Tadjiks and the Sunni Uzbeks, the Armenian Christians and the Azerbaidjan Muslims But generally it was a conflict of nationalities For instance, the Uzbeks and the Turkomans had the same religion as Sunni Muslims, and yet were always fighting with each other. There was no love lost between the White Russians and the Great Russians, although they were of the same Christian persuasion

This conflict of nationalities suited the policy of the Tsar to divide and rule In every province of the Russian Empire were settled different nationalities, with nothing in common between them, in pursuit of this policy The empire was governed in the interests of the Great Russians to whom all other nationalities and peoples were held as inferior and subordinate It was a deliberate policy of ruthless Russification of all non-Russian nationalities dictated by an aggressive and militant Russian nationalism

Contrary Soviet Policy towards Unification of Nationalities: When the Bolsheviks came to power in November, 1917, they saw that their first task was to deal with the national and communal problem which became very acute and dangerous especially after the failure of the provisional government which came into power in March, 1917 to tackle it Disintegrating tendencies were seen in full swing on all sides and these received added strength and emphasis from the slogan of self-determination of which so much was made in the last Great War then in progress The Moslem populations of Russia were influenced by pan Islamic and pan-Turkish movements and were harbouring designs to secede from the new order Similar separatist tendencies also affected the other peoples like the Georgians the Armenians the Ukranians and the White Russians who were all showing symptoms of unrest and ambition to set up in their own independent States A bold stroke of statesmanship was called for to win over the hesitant nationalities to the cause of the Revolution and of Russian unity The new government rose to the occasion and at once issued its policy of reclamation in the following significant and assuring terms 'Mohammeddans of Russia Tatars of the Volga and Crimea Kirghiz and Sartes of Siberia and Turkestan Turks and Tartars of Transcaucasia your beliefs and customs, your national institutions and culture are hereafter free and inviolable You have the right to them Know that your rights as well as those of all the peoples of Russia are under the powerful protection of the Revolution and of the organs of the Soviets for workers soldiers and peasants Lend your support to this Revolution and to its government."

This proclamation had its immediate effect in arresting the disruptive tendencies which had been gaining in strength and volume by assuring self-determination to all the peoples inhabiting the territory of the former Russian Empire. The centripetal forces were rendered stronger than the centrifugal ones A Soviet Commonwealth was now organized in the form of a free Federation of Nationalities Under the constitution of 1918, it was named Russian Socialist Federative Soviet Republic, or RSFSR This proclamation served as a model for the other Socialist Republics established by the Bolsheviks (Ukraine, White Russia, the Transcaucasian Federation, and the Central Asiatic Republic)

Formation of USSR: Pursuant to their adoption of a new Constitution, all these Soviet States were combined into a larger Federation under a new name, the Union of Socialist Soviet Republics, or USSR It is to be noted that the word 'Russian' has been dropped from this name to emphasise the repudiation by the new Federation of any nationalistic predominance or claims of superiority which the word came to connote in the course of history under the Tsarist regime

Its Component Units: The USSR is federated in several superposed degrees, since many of its constitutive units have federal structure themselves Although the various component communities are constituted into separate political units, they do not all possess the same rank within the hierarchical structure The maximum of rights is enjoyed by the National or Union Republics which are eleven in number, as stated above They are possessed of complete autonomy and have a share through their representatives in the joint direction of the USSR They have also the right to "dispose freely of themselves, even to the extent of seceding from the Union" (as confirmed by the Constitution of 1936 in Article 17). The twenty-two Autonomous Republics which are next in rank are not granted the right of self-determination "to the point of secession," but are only "independent in the management of local affairs." Lastly, there is a third category of autonomous formations, comprising autonomous provinces (*oblast*), "national" circuits (*okrug*), "national" districts (*rayon*), and even "national" villages ('national' referring here to racial and linguistic peculiarities). These lesser "national" units vary in number from time to time. Their autonomy is limited to local affairs and is subject to the control of the particular "Union Republic" or the "Autonomous Republic" ruling the territory in which their "enclave" is situated.

Rights of Union Republics: It is to be noted that the Republics of the first category, the eleven National or Union Republics which are also called the "Member-States", and which form the nucleus of the Soviet Union, derive their status and large powers from the following conditions which they fulfil: (1) The nationality after which each such State is named must form a compact majority of its population; (2) Its total population must have a minimum of a million; (3) To acquire the right of secession from the Union, it must be so situated on the frontiers that the secession may be geographically possible. But the Constitution does not envisage the possibility of seceding States forming themselves into other Unions of their own, apart from the USSR.

Regional Reconstruction: Thus the first step that the New Constitution had to take to form and stabilise itself was to reshape its physical basis by a new territorial division determined by the national principle supplemented by geographical and economic considerations. The regional reconstruction aimed at the abolition of the old system under which each Province was the home of several races at constant conflict with one another.

Division of Power Between the Centre and the Units: Broading speaking, the division of powers between the Centre and its constituent Units of different grades is that subjects like Foreign Policy, Defence, Transport, Post and Telegraph are administered by the Union Government; Economic, Financial, and Labour problems are jointly administered by the Union Government and the Member-States; while Law, Public Health, Welfare Organisation, and Education are given over to the local control of the Member-States and the autonomous Republics and Regions. Thus these various Soviets are, within these limits, self-governing units enjoying complete cultural autonomy.

Cultural Autonomy: This new policy of reconstructing Russia on the basis of giving to its different communities cultural autonomy and self-government was not carried out without opposition which was inspired by the old die-hard ideas of a dominant nationalism associated with the Great Russians and their constituent "Union Republic." But the new order stood for the other principle of equality between the different races of Russia and steps for producing this equality by raising the cultural intellectual and economic level of the backward communities and regions through self government as the most potent uplifting agency

The grant of Cultural *Autonomy* has *endeared* all its constituent communities to the Soviet Union Its main programme is that every community will impart instruction to its children in its own language But this was not an easy task at the beginning There were many communities which were so backward that their languages did not develop alphabets The Soviet set up special organisations for introducing alphabets where they were not known and by 1934 they were able to endow as many as 74 communities with their own alphabets Education was also spread among the backward peoples like the Tatars and Mongols by means of nomadic schools travelling libraries and other facilities.

Centralisation The system of the USSR is liable to be *misunderstood in regard to some of its main features* No doubt it stands for a large measure of local liberty and self-determination but it is subject to limitations The concessions to communities and national minorities are so granted that they do not impair the strength of the Union as a whole As observed by the Webbs The State as a whole maintains its unity unimpaired and has even like other federal States increased its centralisation of authority It is only in the USSR that this centralisation involves no lessening of the cultural autonomy of the minorities

Limits to Local Autonomy Even as regards local self government an examination of its content from the strictly legal point of view will show that it does not amount to much in practice and substance In practice, the local autonomy is very much reduced by the system which is based on the overlapping of the various superposed administrative organs, between whose different spheres of jurisdiction there is hardly any clear and defined line of demarcation

No doubt, the Regulations (of October 16, 1929) governing Village Soviets, and those for Town Soviets (of October 24, 1925) seem to confer upon these bodies wide powers But the same wide powers are given to the immediate superior authority over the Village or Town Soviet, *viz*, that of the District, and, above the District, to the still higher authority of the Province The District and Provincial Regulations issued at different dates in 1928 and 1929 make these higher bodies responsible for all the services in the villages and towns situated in their respective areas which are supposed to be the special concern of the Village and Town Soviets "Had the list of obligations incumbent on the authorities of a given village or town been imposed exclusively on them, neither the Central Government nor any of the intermediary bodies would have had any thing to do for that particular village or town except in respect of foreign relations and national defence" (N de Basily *Russia Under Soviet Rule*, p 161)

In the Soviet system, a higher administrative body can supersede that just below it and take over its functions for which the lower body is not made exclusively responsible The responsibility is shared by both It is a dual government The superior administrative organ has also even the right to object to the election or nomination of a functionary and to dismiss him. There is in fact, no sphere which an inferior administrative body can call its own as its exclusive sphere of independent action Thus the local executives function under a "double subordination' "In these circumstances it is impossible to speak of local autonomy in the sovietic State What is designated by this term is merely a deceptive resemblance of administrative decentralisation In other words every local government matter is assumed to be a function of the Central Government but as it is materially impossible for the latter to assume the burden of them all a vast proportion of its duties are delegated to various executive committees or to sections of these which by the play of the system of double subordination' become so many local agents of the Central Government

Extent of Centralisation Thus there are no real local authorities throughout the Soviet State On the contrary it is a State in which centralisation has been pushed to its extreme logical limits From this point of view the Constitution of 1936 has brought nothing new All it does is change in the method of composing the local Assemblies from the Province to the Village' (*Ib* pp 162 163)

The clauses of the Constitution show that the powers reserved for the Federal Government are very wide and left vague and undefined The fundamental fact is also to be considered that the basis of the Constitution is its economic plan which comprehends within its all-embracing scope, the entire life of the country and all its parts This economic plan falls exclusively within the sphere of the federal administration. This, together with the structure of society as described in Chapter I. and the Basic Rights and Duties of Citizens as defined in Chapter X, offer unlimited scope for interference by the federal authorities with the organs of local government Article 15, which seemingly limits federal powers, in practice only safeguards the rights of communities to "cultural autonomy" and specially to the use of local languages On the other hand, Articles 20, 49(c), 68(a), 69 and 87 give to the superior authorities the right to disallow and cancel the orders of the local authorities where these are against the Constitution or the federal laws.

The Constitution of 1936 gives the USSR the stamp of a "State" proper, "with one foreign policy, one united army, one social system, and one general type of government for all its parts" Lenin is alleged to have attributed to Stalin "Great Russian chauvinism", and the new Constitution under Stalin's influence is believed by its critics to be a "menace to the USSR as a federal union" and they anticipate for the future, instead of greater autonomy for its parts, and an increase in the number of constituent republics, a new policy of consolidation, so that it may again become "Russia, one and indivisible" (Hawgood: *Modern Constitutions.* p. 402)

Right of Secession Confined only to Eleven Primary Republics and not Allowed as a General Right: Along with the true content and extent of local autonomy in the Soviet system, the right of secession it has granted to its constituent units is liable to be misunderstood in its implications and practical bearings In the first place it is to be noted that this right is not a fundamental feature of the Soviet Constitution It is not a general right which the Constitution confers on all its Units It is restricted only to eleven Units the National Republics It is not granted to the numerous other units the many Autonomous Republics and Regions Even as regards the right which is restricted to the eleven States it was forced by circumstances The position will be clear from the following remarks of Stalin "The attitude of the Communist Party towards the right of secession was determined by the concrete factors of the international situation, by the interests of the Revolution This is why the Communists fight for the secession of the colonies from the *Entente* but they must at the same time fight against the severance of border regions from Russia Three years before in 1917 Stalin stated When we recognise the right of oppressed peoples to secede the right to determine their political destiny we do not thereby settle the question whether particular nations should secede from the Russian State at the given moment

Thus we are at liberty to agitate for or against the secession according to the interests of the proletariat of the proletarian revolution' Another point to be noted in this connexion is that "during the Purge of 1937 38 there were several references in the Press to men who were accused of plotting to bring about secession of some territory from the Union Such activities have been invariably interpreted by Soviet

Court as treasonable and counter-revolutionary. It is, therefore, perfectly clear that the exercise of the right of secession is effectively prevented by the structure of the Soviet State and the Communist Doctrine that governs it"

Stalin's Speech on the Subject: More light is thrown on the subject by Stalin in the memorable speech he delivered on November 14, 1936 on the New Constitution with reference to Article 17 of the Draft Constitution and the Amendment that was proposed to it. The Amendment proposed was to delete from the Constitution Article 17 which reserved to the Union Republics the right of free secession from the USSR On this Amendment, Stalin made the following pertinent remarks "It is said that there is not a single republic in the USSR that wants to secede from the USSR and that, therefore, Article 17 is of no practical importance It is, of course, true that not a single republic wants to secede from the USSR. But this does not, in the least, mean that we ought not fix in the Constitution the right of Union Republics freely to secede from the USSR In the USSR, there is not a single Union Republic that wants to oppress another Union Republic. But this does not, in the least, mean that we ought to delete from the Constitution of the USSR the Article dealing with the equality of rights of the Union Republics" Stalin also dwelt on a proposal that "on reaching the proper level of economic and cultural development, the Autonomous Soviet Socialist Republics may be transformed into Union Soviet Socialist Republics" It is to be recalled that by such a promotion in their status the Autonomous Republics would acquire the right given to the Union Republics to secede from the Union of SSR This was precisely the ground on which the proposal was turned down Stalin explained this point thus

> What are the grounds for transferring Autonomous Republics to the category of Union Republics?
>
> There are three such grounds
>
> *First* the Republic in question must be a border Re public a Republic that is not surrounded on all sides by USSR territory Why? Because since the Union Republics have the right to secede from the USSR a Republic on becoming a Union Republic must be able logically and in fact to raise the question of its seceding from the USSR And this question can be raised only by a Republic which say borders on some foreign State and consequently is not surrounded on all sides by USSR territory *Of course none of our Republics would actually raise the question of seceding from the USSR* But since the right to secede from the USSR is reserved to the Union Republics it must be so arranged that this right does not become a meaningless scrap of paper Take for example the Bashkir Republic or the Tartar Republic Let us assume that these Autonomous Republics aro transferred to the category of Union Re publics Could they logically and in fact raise the question of seceding from the USSR? No they could not. Why? Because they are surrounded on all sides by Soviet Republics and Regions and strictly speaking they have nowhere to go to if they secede from the USSR (laughter and applause) Therefore it would be wrong to transfer such Republics to the category of Union Republics.

This shows that the right to secede carried with it fundamental geographical conditions by which it may be negatived

"*Secondly*, the nationality which gives its name to a given Soviet Republic must constitute a more or less compact majority within that Republic. Take the Crimean Autonomous Republic, for example It is a border republic, but the Crimean Tatars do not constitute the majority in that republic; on the contrary, they are a minority Consequently, it would be wrong and illogical to transfer the Crimean Republic to the category of Union Republics"

This means that no Minority can be given the right to secede on behalf of the State to which it belongs

"*Thirdly*, the republic must not have too small a population, it should have a population of, say, not less but more than a million, at least Why? Because it would be wrong to assume that a small Soviet Republic with a very small population and a small army could hope to maintain an independent State existence There can hardly be any doubt that the imperialist beasts of prey would soon grab it"

This furnishes an excellent commentary on the extravagances of separatist demands started in India for creating Provinces without reference to the primary factor of their financial and military self-sufficiency

Thus the USSR had to form itself by giving the right to secede to its 11 Constituent Republics representing its nucleus to rope them in They were induced to vote themselves into the Union, but now that they are in the Union, they have no desire to vote themselves out of it and are themselves making the Union more and more centralized

Again, since the USSR is a multi-national State, the cultural and regional autonomy for all its Units is the only form of political structure which may suit such a State and keep together its diverse elements

India however has been spared this process of her political development as a Union India as an integral unity is not something that is in the process of making It has been already made It is a living reality before our eyes and has been administered as such for over a century by the present Government of India which maintains its paramount sovereignty equally over all the Provinces and States of India and has subjected them to its irresistible process of unification Should we now begin by going back upon that history as is being persistently pressed by a particular community? Should the British also encourage this new idea of separatism and still seek to divide and rule and destroy their greatest gift to India its unity? We should rather begin by assuming the Indian Union and taking it as our starting point We should not think of divorce before marriage

The Viceroy's Declaration Against Pakistan. It is a matter of great gratification that the latest declaration of its policy by the British Government made through the Viceroy in the speech he delivered the other day (in December 1942) in Calcutta recognises the need of building India s constitution on the foundation of her geographical unity The Viceroy further pointed out that there should not be a divided military command for India and that with her integral unity preserved she should speak with one voice in the expression of foreign policy at the Comity of Nations

Causes of Present Political Deadlock: Indeed, the Pakistan issue is not being discussed in the light of all its realities and results It has been proposed as a permanent settlement of the communal problem But it goes much farther and creates other more difficult problems, as envisaged by Gandhiji. Indeed, the present political deadlock is due to the disagreement of the two major political parties of India, the Moslem League, and the Congress, on this issue. The Cripps' Scheme offered (1) the possibility of Pakistan and (2) that on a general plebiscite The Moslem League wants (1) an immediate guarantee of Pakistan and (2) Moslem Plebiscite to decide it. The Congress is opposed to Pakistan on principle Its position is thus put by Mahatma Gandhi · "If Pakistan is an article of faith with Mr Jinnah, indivisibility of India is an article of faith with me Hence there is stalemate" Besides, Gandhiji sees in Pakistan the following implications (1) "It is a demand for carving out of India a portion to be treated as a wholly independent and sovereign State (2) This sovereign State can conceivably go to war against the one of which it was but yesterday a part (3) It can also equally conceivably make treaties with other States" The Congress in this matter also represents the entire Hindu opinion

It may be solved by USSR Scheme of Communal Cultural Autonomy: These two diametrically opposed views may, however, be reconciled by the way shown by the USSR in dealing with its more difficult communal problems, by its scheme of the cultural autonomy of communities by which, as we have seen, it has brought and kept together within its vast Union so many different communities, nationalities and regions whose differences are much more fundamental than the differences between the Hindus and Moslems of India This comprehensive principle has bound together all the communities of the USSR in ties of a common Soviet citizenship and nationalism and rendered the Union a living entity which is now acquitting itself so well in defending the freedom of their common Mother Country

Thus this Scheme is the only conceivable one by which the independence of communities can be granted without destroying the integrity of the Mother Country as a whole and its place and power in World Politics

It is also the Canadian Scheme There is another case of a Constitution which bears closely upon the constitutional problems of India It is that of the Dominion of Canada As is well known Canada had been long torn by acute divisions between the English and the French in Canada With their deep differences in religion and historic traditions the two Canadas became at last united into one State mainly on the basis of the above scheme of Cultural Autonomy for each of the two communities English and French

The initial difficulty in Canada which obstructed her progress towards a self governing constitution was the permanent and seemingly irreconcilable antagonism between the French and the English in point of religion language and historical experience and tradition The French Canadians are all Roman Catholics and unambitious and content with the domestic joys afforded by their homes their occupations their reli gion and their province The English Canadians follow the Protestant religion, and are energetic and ambitious," with their special industrial, commercial, maritime and financial interests, as distinguished from the predominantly rival interests of the French "And yet, despite these differences in race, language, religion and outlook on life, no other provinces in the Dominion have achieved so much in common politically"

But this political unity was not achieved at the sacrifice of any essential cultural interests A system of separate, sectarian schools was one of the legacies of the Dominion There were permitted separate schools for Roman Catholics as well as for Protestants out of public funds, though the opinion of the majority of the people was against the separate schools and was for a common school system On the eve of the Confederation, out of 4,000 schools in Upper Canada, 100 were separate schools, Roman Catholic in management, organisation, atmosphere and teaching Accordingly, the fathers of the Confederation felt compelled to acknowledge this system in the new Constitution It is embodied in Section 98 of the British North America Act It gives the right of separate schools both to the Catholics and to the Protestants Only it must be noted that the separate school system is operative in only two out of the nine Provinces of the Dominion In these, the Education Act adopted declares "the school system shall be conducted upon strictly non-sectarian principles Books inculcating the highest morality shall be selected for the use of such schools and all books of a religious character teaching denominational dogma, shall be strictly excluded therefrom" The contention over separate schools has been occasionally very acute and produced several crises in Canadian politics and even considerable amount of litigation, but eventually the people got reconciled to it as one of the conditions of the Confederation

It is also the Scheme of the League of Nations The underlying principle behind the separate schools system has now been recognised by the League of Nations though in a different form The League stands for the protection of the religious racial and linguistic interests of Minorities where they form ' considerable proportion of the population and grants special schools out of public funds where they are claimed by a sufficient number of pupils 40 in the case of elementary and 300 for secondary schools

Canada is more unitary than USA It may also be noted that the fathers of Canadian Federation found in the American Civil War certain elements of weakness and danger in the USA Constitution which they wanted to avoid They aimed at a Federal Union having a Constitution which would reduce the likelihood of friction between the Central Government and the different provincial administrations They therefore wanted to strengthen the Central Government in the Canadian Constitution and to confer on the provincial bodies only such powers as were required for local purposes instead of creating them as so many distinct sovereignties The Dominion of Canada was therefore planned as a Unitary State with its residuary powers resting in the Centre and not in its Units Perhaps the supposed defects of the

USA Constitution were somewhat exaggerated at that time, because certain changes have been since made in that Constitution which have strengthened the restraints upon State-Legislatures and made these enforceable by the Supreme Court President Taft even feared that a "great widening of the field of federal activity and a substantial diminution of State-rights would in the end threaten the integrity of the Union instead of promoting it" According to President Woodrow Wilson, "government with us has ceased to be plural and has become singular, the Government of the United States. Distinct as are its parts, they are not separate"

Thus it may be taken for granted that the present trend in the USA Constitution is towards strengthening the Centre as the symbol of a single nationhood, just as in the USSR there is the same trend towards greater and greater centralization and making the bonds by which its different parts are related to the Union closer and stronger, while the Dominion of Canada more unreservedly emphasises its central unity and strength, without encroaching unduly upon the legitimate spheres of provincial autonomy

Alternatives to Pakistan: Coming now to the bearings of these important Western Federations upon the problems of India, it goes without saying that Pakistan represents an extreme step for solving communal problems, even at the cost of destroying the unity of the mother country and the integrity of the parent State Its advocates blind themselves to the fact that Pakistan is already operative in all the four Muslim Majority provinces They are now out to get rid of the Indian Union on the ground that such a Union with a Hindu majority will override the sovereignty of a Pakistan province But the solution of this difficulty is quite feasible within the Union and without partitioning the parent State

There are several ways to this solution The first is so to frame the Schedules of Federal and Provincial subjects as to make the most of provincial autonomy and to render each Pakistan a sovereign State for all practical purposes

The second solution is to guarantee to each community its cultural autonomy on the lines on which its scheme is worked in the USSR This scheme is an amplification in actual practice of the scheme which the League of Nations had framed for the protection of Minorities as a part of international law Details of the scheme have been already given above

There is a third way by which communities may reconcile themselves to a common Federation without parting from one another and partitioning the country into separate States of their own It is to reconstitute the provinces as linguistic units provided they are financially self supporting The King Emperor in annulling the Partition of Bengal promised a Boundaries Commission for the purpose but his gracious promise has remained unredeemed Bengal has suffered most by losing vast Bengali speaking areas to her neighbouring Provinces while Orissa has been justly created as a linguistic province

In these circumstances, is it too much to hope that the League may be induced to try to explore the possibilities of other plans for a settlement without going to the extreme of splitting up the unity of India into any number of warring States, with Minority problems still in hot pursuit, to boot?

The view of the Muslim League (which its President, Mr Jinnah, was pleased to explain to me personally) is that "the safeguards, constitutional or otherwise, will be of no use, so long as there is a communal Hindu majority at the Centre, the safeguards will only remain on paper" It is not difficult to discover a device by which these doubts may be solved The rights of Minorities, under this scheme of the cultural autonomy of communities, will be protected by law and the constitution The Constitution may set up a separate legal machinery to deal with and enforce the safeguards it grants to the Minorities, like the Supreme Court to which an aggrieved community will be at liberty to take its grievances The composition of such a Supreme Court need not be communal The Hindus have never objected to the present composition of India's Federal Court where there is already an equality of representation in the personnel of its judges as between the Hindus and the Moslems

The Moslem League Daily called *Dawn* in a recent editorial has sought to answer my proposals regarding feasible alternatives to Pakistan by stating that the safeguards for Minorities cannot be trusted to the keeping of a completely sovereign body like the Federal Legislature with its Hindu majority which can at its own sweet will cancel these safeguards or even pack the Supreme Court with its own partisans The reply to that is that the Indian Union will be the product of an agreement or treaty between the parties concerned like the Irish Free State and that the Supreme Court will always be non communal in its composition as the protector of the rights of Minorities

The trend of Politics is towards World Federation resting on the Principle of Non violence The present trend of politics is thus inevitably towards larger and larger aggregates towards larger Unions of States and even Unions of Empires and ultimately towards a World Union The appointed destiny of Mankind is a world order based upon Universal Peace to be achieved and sustained by a living sense of its unity as an integral part of its political consciousness It must outgrow the system by which it is splitting up into any number of warring nations Peace cannot be produced by Violence Man must evolve the international mind Western thought has so far culminated in power politics in the unabashed rule of Might against Right Human evolution has been a part of *general biological evolution shaped by Nature red* in tooth and claw Nature has ordained that the world must pass through a painful historical development from the brute to the man But should the Ascent of Man be inevitably a blood process? The path of Violence leads but to Violence and more of Violence There seems to be now a retrogression in human evolution The world is overwhelmed by forces of rebarbarization turning whole continents into armed hostile and war ring camps. The salvation of humanity can result only from a completely contrary ideology That ideology is more eastern than western. The turning point in human evolution can be given only by Indian thought based on non-violence, *Ahimsa* as *parama-dharma*, the supreme religion of mankind. The starting-point of Indian thought is that God is in every creature and particle of the Universe, breathes life into it, and pervades it at every point so that, as the Upanishads state, nothing is beside Him, the Brahman Thus, violence to God's creature is violence towards God, a denial of God. Therefore, non-violence in this view becomes the only possible religion of mankind India has sought to stand for this religion, and for once even applied it in the sphere of politics. It was done by one of her Kings, Asoka (C 274-235 B C) whom H G Wells counts as the greatest king in history Asoka is never tired of preaching in his many sermons on stone, in his proclamations inscribed on pillars, and the rocks of ages, the doctrine of peace which he extended to mean not merely peace between man and man but between man and every sentient creature, while in politics he bravely based his large empire of a Greater India extending from Persia to Southern India upon the principle of Non-Violence and declared for a policy of what is termed in the Sanskrit political treatises, *Dharma-Vijaya*, spiritual conquest, a conquest achieved by love (*priti*) and not by Violence As a result of this policy, the conquest of only one province, that of Kalinga, came to be his only annexation. The colossal carnage of that conquest won by force against a brave people who had hitherto remained "unconquered" (*avijita*) produced in Asoka s mind a complete reaction from the cult of Violence to that of Non Violence Henceforth Asoka stood out as the Pioneer of Peace in the world of his days and sent out from India his Peace Missions instead of expeditionary military forces to extend an aggressive imperialism These Peace Missions were despatched by him to the then leading States of the west such as Syria under Antiochus II Egypt under Ptolemy Philadelphos Cyrene under Magas Epirus under Alexander and Macedonia under Antigonas and were equipped with measures for relief of suffering in pursuit of Asoka s policy of Universal Brotherhood based on Non Violence But Asoka was too far ahead of his age and humanity is still too far from realization of his ideals which he had so effectively translated into action The world is in need of India and of her message which one of her greatest sons Mahatma Gandhi has done so much to revive and enforce India should now have full and unfettered freedom to effec tively present before the world the message she has carried through history the message of Non Violence as the only basis upon which a stable world-order can be built up The next step in human evolution must inevitably be Non Violence inspired by an abiding sense of the fundamental unity of mankind and of all life

APPENDIX I

SELECT ARTICLES OF THE USSR CONSTITUTION

ARTICLE 13

The Union of Soviet Socialist Republics is a federated State, formed on the basis of the voluntary association of Soviet Socialist Republics possessing equal rights, namely,

The Russian Soviet Federative Socialist Republic
The Ukrainian Soviet Socialist Republic
The Byelorussian Soviet Socialist Republic
The Azerbaidjan Soviet Socialist Republic
The Georgian Soviet Socialist Republic
The Armenian Soviet Socialist Republic
The Turkmen Soviet Socialist Republic
The Uzbek Soviet Socialist Republic
The Tadjik Soviet Socialist Republic
The Kazakh Soviet Socialist Republic
The Kirghiz Soviet Socialist Republic

ARTICLE 14

The jurisdiction of the Union of Soviet Socialist Republics, as represented by its highest organs of power and organs of state administration, covers

(a) Representation of the Union in international relations, conclusion and ratification of treaties with other States·

(b) Questions of War and Peace,

(c) Admission of new republics into the USSR,

(d) Supervision over the observance of the Constitution of the USSR and ensuring that the Constitutions of the Union Republics conform with the Constitution of the USSR

(e) Ratification of alterations of boundaries between Union Republics

(f) Ratification of the formation of new Territories and Regions and also of new Autonomous Republics within the Union Republics

(g) Organisation of the defence of the USSR and the direction of all the armed forces of the USSR,

(h) Foreign trade on the basis of state monopoly

(i) Safeguarding the security of the State,

(j) Determining the plans of national economy of the USSR

(k) Approval of the unified State Budget of the USSR as well as of the taxes and revenues which go to form the Union Republican and local Budgets

(l) Administration of the banks industrial and agricultural establishments and enterprises, and trading enterprises of all Union importance,

(m) Administration of transport and communications

(n) Direction of the monetary and credit system,

(o) Organisation of State insurance

(p) Contracting and granting loans

(q) Establishment of the basic principles of land tenure as well as of the use of mineral deposits forests and waters

(r) Establishment of the basic principles in the spheres of education and public health,

(s) Organisation of a uniform system of national economic accounting,

(t) Establishment of the principles of labour legislation,

(u) Legislation governing the judicial system and judicial procedure, Criminal and Civil Codes;

(v) Laws governing citizenship of the Union, Laws governing the rights of foreigners,

(w) Issuance of all-Union acts of amnesty

ARTICLE 21

One Union citizenship is established for all citizens of the USSR

Every citizen of a Union Republic is a citizen of the USSR

ARTICLE 22

The Russian Soviet Federative Socialist Republic consists of the Azov-Black Sea, Far-Eastern, West Siberian, Krassnoyarsk and North Caucasian *Territories*, the Voronezh, East Siberian, Gorky, Western, Ivanovo, Kalinin, Kirov, Kuibyshev, Kursk, Leningrad, Moscow, Omsk, Orenburg, Saratov, Sverdlovsk, Northern, Stalingard, Chelyabinsk and Yaroslavl *Regions*; the Tatar, Bashkir, Daghestan, Buryat-Mongolian, Kabardino-Balkarian, Kalmyk, Karelian, Komi, Crimean, Mari, Mordovian, Volga German, North Ossetian, Udmurt, Chechen-Ingush, Chuvash and Yakut *Autonomous Soviet Socialist Republics*, the Adygei,

Jewish Karachai Oirot Khakass and Cherkess *Autonomous Regions*

ARTICLE 23

The Ukranian Soviet Socialist Republic consists of the Vinnitsa Dniepropetrovsk, Donetz, Kiev, Odessa, Kharkov and Chernigov *Regions* and the Moldavian *Autonomous Soviet Socialist Republic*

ARTICLE 24

The Azerbaidjan Soviet Socialist Republic includes the Nakhichevan Autonomous Soviet Socialist Republic and the Nagorno-Karabakh Autonomous Region

ARTICLE 25

The Georgian Soviet Socialist Republic includes the Abkhazian Autonomous Soviet Socialist Republic the Adjar Autonomous Soviet Socialist Republic and the South Ossetian Autonomous Region

ARTICLE 26

The Uzbek Soviet Socialist Republic includes the Kara Kalpak Autonomous Soviet Socialist *Republic*

ARTICLE 27

The Tadjik Soviet Socialist Republic includes the Gorno-Badakhshan Autonomous *Region*

ARTICLE 28

The Kazakh Soviet Socialist Republic consists of the Aktyubinsk Alma ata East Kazaghstan West Kazakh stan Karaganda Kustanai North Kazakhstan and South Kazakhstan *Regions*

ARTICLE 29

The Armenian Soviet Socialist Republic, the Byelorussian Soviet Socialist Republic, the Turkmen Soviet Socialist Republic, and the Kirghiz Soviet Socialist Republic contain no Autonomous Republics or Territories and *Regions*

ARTICLE 35

The Soviet of Nationalities is elected by the citizens of the USSR according to Union and Autonomous Republics, Autonomous Regions and National Areas on the basis of twenty-five deputies from each Union Republic, eleven deputies from each Autonomous Republic, five deputies from each Autonomous Region and one deputy from each National Area.

ARTICLE 37

The two Chambers of the Supreme Soviet of the USSR, the Soviet of the Union, and the Soviet of Nationalities, have equal rights

ARTICLE 39

A law is deemed to be adopted if passed by both Chambers of the Supreme Soviet of the USSR by a simple majority in each.

APPENDIX II

EXTRACTS FROM THE WRITINGS OF STALIN

1 'Any mistrust of Russia which existed among the peoples was fostered chiefly by the policy of Tsarism But now that Tsarism no longer exists its policy of oppression no longer exists this mistrust is bound to diminish and the attraction towards Russia increase I believe that now after the overthrow of Tsarism, nine-tenths of the peoples will not desire secession. The Party therefore proposes to institute regional autonomy for regions which may not desire secession and which are distinguished by peculiarities of social life and language as for instance Transcaucasia Turkestan and the Ukraine The geographical boundaries of these autonomous regions shall be determined by the population itself with due regard for the exigencies of economic life social life etc
(P 162 Stalin s *Kampf*)

2 Soviet autonomy is the most real and concrete way of uniting the border regions to Central Russia Nobody will deny that the Ukraine, Azerbaidjan Turkestan the Kirghiz Republic the Bashkir Republic the Tatar Republic and other border regions since they are striving for the cultural and material prosperity of their masses must have their native schools courts administration and government bodies recruited principally from among the native peoples *Furthermore* the real sovietization of these regions their conversion into Soviet countries closely bound to Central Russia and forming with it one state whole is *inconceivable* with

out the widespread organization of local schools, without the creation of courts, administrative bodies, organs of government, etc., recruited from among people acquainted with the life and language of the population. But to conduct the schools, courts, the administration and organs of government in the native language means precisely putting Soviet autonomy into practice; for Soviet autonomy is but the sum of these various institutions enveloped in a Ukranian, Turkestanian or Kirghiz form (*Ib.* p 175)

3 There are three groups of circumstances which render the amalgamation of the Soviet Republics into a single Confederate State inevitable.

The first group consists of facts relating to the internal economic situation Firstly, there is the meagreness of the economic resources remaining at the disposal of the Republics after years of war, which obliges us to combine these meagre resources so as to employ them more rationally and to develop the main branches of production, those which form the backbone of Soviet power in each Republic Second, there is the historically determined natural division of labour, the economic division of labour, between the various Regions, and Republics of our Federation. For instance, the North supplies the South and East with textiles, the South and East supply the North with cotton, fuel and so forth The division of labour thus established between the Regions cannot be eliminated by a mere stroke of the pen it has been created historically by the whole course of economic development of the Federation And this division of labour, which renders the full development of individual Regions impossible so long as the Republics lead separate existence is oblig ing our Republics to knit themselves into a single economic unit Thirdly, there is the fact that the principal means of communication in the Federation, which are the nerve and backbone of any possible Union, consti tute a single system It goes without saying that the means of communication cannot be left in a divided state in the hands of, and subordinated to, the interests of the individual Republics *for that would convert the* main nerve of economic life—transport—into a conglomeration of separate parts utilized without regard to plan This circumstance also induces the Republics to favour amalgamation into a single State Finally, there is the meagreness of our financial resources

The second group of circumstances rendering the amalgamation of the Republics essential consists of facts relating to our international position

The danger of attack from without demands that our military front should be absolutely united, that our army should be an absolutely united army There is again a danger of the economic isolation of our Federation This danger is to be met by the creation of a united economic front of our Soviet Republics in face of the capitalist encirclement.

There is also the danger of an organised diplomatic boycott or isolation of our Federation Hence the necessity for a united front along diplomatic lines also (*Ib* pp 177 179)

4 Within the Soviet Union there are about 60 nations, national groups, and nationalities. The Soviet State is a multi-national State Clearly, the question of the relations between the peoples of the USSR cannot but be one of first-rate importance for us (p 187, *Ib.*)

APPENDIX III

ARTICLE 93 OF THE CANADIAN CONSTITUTION ON EDUCATION

In and for each Province the Legislature may exclusively make laws in relation to Education, subject and according to the following provisions

(1) Nothing in any such Law shall prejudicially affect any Right or Privilege with respect to Denominational Schools which any Class of Persons have by Law in the Province at the Union

(2) All the Powers Privileges and Duties at the Union by Law conferred and imposed in Upper Canada on the Separate Schools and School Trustees of the Queen s Roman Catholic Subjects shall be and the same are hereby extended to the Dissentient Schools of the Queen s Protestant and Roman Catholic subjects in Quebec

(3) Where in any Province a System of Separate or Dissentient Schools exists by Law at the Union or is thereafter established by the Legislature of the Province an Appeal shall lie to the Governor General in Council from any Act or Decision of any Provincial Authority affecting any Right or Privilege of the Protestant or Roman Catholic Minority of the Queen s subjects in relation to Education.

APPENDIX IV.

FUNDAMENTAL RIGHTS FROM SELECT CONSTITUTIONS

I

1. The Liberty of the Person is inviolable, and no person will be deprived of liberty except in law.

2 The dwelling of every person is inviolable and shall not be forcibly entered except in accordance with law

3 Freedom of conscience and the free profession and practice of religion are, subject to public order and morality, guaranteed to every citizen

4 The right of free expression of opinion as well as the right to assemble peaceably and without arms, and to form Associations or Unions is guaranteed for purposes not opposed to public morality. Laws regulating the manner in which the right of forming associations and the right of free assembly may be exercised shall contain no political, religious, or class distinction (*Irish Free State*)

II

1 There shall be but one nationality in the country All citizens shall be equal before the law.

2 The liberty of the individual shall be guaranteed

3 No person may be tried save by a competent court

4 No person may be subjected to any judicial interrogation or placed under arrest or be in any other way deprived of his liberty, save as provided by law

No person may be placed under arrest for any crime or offence whatever save by order of a competent authority given in writing and stating the charge This order must be communicated to the person arrested at the time of arrest or at latest within twenty four hours of the arrest An appeal against the order for arrest may be lodged in the competent court within three days If no appeal has been lodged within this period the police authorities must as a matter of course communicate the order to the competent court within the twenty four hours following The court shall be bound to confirm or annul the arrest within two days from the communication of the order and its decision shall be given effect forthwith

Public officials who infringe these provisions shall be punished for illegal deprivation of liberty

5 No person may be tried without having been previously interrogated by the competent authority or having been afforded an opportunity by legal means to defend himself

6 Every dwelling shall be inviolable

7 Liberty of Religion and of conscience shall be guaranteed All recognized religions shall be equal before the law and may be practised in public

8 The enjoyment of civil and political rights shall be independent of the practice of any religion.

9. Recognized religions shall within the limits of the law be self-governing as regards the regulation of their internal affairs and the administration of their funds and endowments.

10 So far as the State Budgets may provide funds for religious purposes, these funds shall be divided amongst the various recognized religious bodies in proportion to the numbers of their adherents and according to their actual proved necessities

11. Citizens shall have the right to form associations, to assemble in meetings and to take collective action (*Czecho-Slovakia*)

III

1 The State guarantees (within its territory) full protection for life, liberty and property to all its inhabitants without distinction of origin, nationality, language, race or religion

2 All citizens are equal before the law Public-employments are open in the same degree to all, under conditions prescribed by law.

3 Within the territory of the State every citizen is free to choose his domicile or place of residence, to change his domicile or emigrate, to choose his profession or means of livelihood, and also to transfer his property

4 Citizens have the right of meeting and of association as well as that of founding societies and unions.

5 Every citizen possesses the right of safeguarding his nationality and of cultivating his national language and customs

Special laws of the State guarantee the full and free development of their national customs to minorities aided by autonomous federations of minorities to which statutory recognition may be given within the limits governing general autonomous federations

In respect of such federations the State is entitled to control and, if necessary is bound to supplement, their financial resources

6 The nationals belonging to minorities in the nation whether based on religion or language have equal rights with other citizens in forming controlling and administering at their own expense charitable religious and social institutions schools and other educational establishments with the free use of their language and practice of their religion therein

7 Liberty of conscience and religion is guaranteed to all nationals No one can be restricted in the exercise of rights accorded to other nationals by reason of his religion or of his religious convictions

All inhabitants of the State have the right freely to practise their form of belief in public or in private and to conform to the precepts and rites of their religion in so far as the practice thereof is not opposed to public order or morality (*Poland*)

IV

1 There shall be a provincial citizenship for each province Federal citizenship shall be acquired by the act of acquiring provincial citizenship Every citizen of the Federation shall have in each province the same

rights and duties as the citizens of the province. (*Austria*)

V

1. Liberty to establish and change one's place of dwelling is guaranteed by the State

Restrictions may also be placed upon this right by other authorities, for reasons of public health, in such cases and in such manner as may be prescribed by law.

2 All persons are free to assemble peaceably and unarmed. All citizens have the right to form association The right to strike is assured.

3 Freedom to choose one's occupation as well as to originate enterprises or industries of an agricultural, commercial, industrial or other nature, is guaranteed by the State No person may be deprived of this right, save in accordance with and subject to the limits laid down by the law

4 Racial minorities in the country have the right to establish autonomous institutions for the preservation and development of their national culture and to maintain special organizations for their welfare, so far as is not incompatible with the interests of the State

5. In districts where the majority of the population belongs to a racial minority, the language used in the administration of local self-governing authorities may be the language of that racial minority, but every citizen has the right to use the language of the State in dealing with such authorities Local self-governing bodies which use the language of a racial minority must use the national language in their communications

with governmental institutions and with other local self governing bodies which do not make use of the language of the same racial minority (*Esthonia*)

VI

1 Every person shall be free within the limits permitted by law to express his opinions by speech writing print picture or other similar means

2 Liberty of conscience and of religion shall be guaranteed.

3 Every inhabitant shall enjoy in the same degree as nationals of the State the right to practise in public or in private any faith religion or creed whatsoever, so far as the practice thereof does not violate the law or public order and morality

4 All religions shall be equal before the law

5 The exercise of certain religious practices may be prohibited if they are contrary to public order or morality

6 (i) All citizens shall be in all respects equal before the law and shall enjoy the same civil and political rights without distinction of race language or religion

(ii) Differences of religion creed, faith or language shall not prejudice any citizen of the State in any way within the limits laid down by general laws particularly in regard to public employment office or honours and to the exercise of any trade or calling

(iii) All citizens of the State may within the limits laid down by general laws freely use any language whatsoever, whether in private or business affairs or in matters of religion, in the Press, or in publications of any kind, or in public meetings.

7. Inasmuch as citizens are entitled in accordance with general laws to establish, manage and administer, at their own expense, religious, charitable and social institutions, schools and other educational establishments, all citizens, without distinction of nationality, language, religion or race, shall be on an equality and shall have the right to the free use of their own language and the free exercise of their own religion in such institutions.

8. In towns and districts where a minority speaks a language other than that of the majority, facilities shall be guaranteed, within the limits laid down by general educational legislation, to enable the children of such minority to receive instruction in the official language Instruction in the State language may at the same time be made obligatory

9. In towns and districts where a considerable proportion of citizens belong to a minority as regards race, religion or language, and where sums of public money are set aside for educational purposes in the State or municipal budgets or otherwise, a due share in the allocation and use of such sums shall be accorded to such minorities, within the limits of the general regulations concerning public administration (*Czecho Slovak Republic*).

VII

1 All inhabitants of the country must enjoy full liberty of faith and of conscience The undisturbed

practice of religion is guaranteed by the Constitution and is under State protection.

2 Civil and political rights and duties are neither dependent upon nor restricted by the practice of religious freedom.

The enjoyment of civil and political rights, as well as admission to official posts, are independent of religious creed.

No one is bound to disclose his religious convictions *(German)*

VIII

1 Alongside the socialist system of economy which is the predominant form of economy in the USSR the law permits small private economy of individual peasants and handicraftsmen based on their personal labour and precluding the exploitation of the labour of others

2 The right of citizens to personal property in their income from work and in their savings in their dwelling houses and auxiliary household economy their domestic furniture and utensils and objects of personal use and comfort as well as the right of inheritance of personal property of citizens are protected by law

3 The citizens of the USSR are guaranteed by law,

(a) freedom of speech

(b) freedom of the press

(c) freedom of assembly and of holding mass meetings

(d) freedom of street processions and demonstrations

These rights of citizens are ensured by placing at the disposal of the toilers and their organizations printing presses, stocks of paper, public buildings, the streets, means of communication and other material requisites for the exercise of these rights.

4. Citizens of the USSR are ensured the right to unite in public organizations—trade unions, co-operative associations, youth organizations, sport and defence organizations, cultural, technical and scientific societies (*USSR*).

5 The list of fundamental rights granted to its citizens by the Stalin Constitution does not include the most elementary of such rights, the right of freedom of moving from place to place, freedom of circulation, or free choice of one's place of residence The Constitution assigns everyone to a given domicile and a place of labour to which he remains tied. All industrial workers are attached to their factories or warehouses which they cannot leave except by permission of their managers. Before 1936 there was introduced a regime of internal passports which had to be furnished with special visa before a citizen of the USSR could be absent from home even for twenty-four hours Permission to cross the frontier and pay a visit abroad is almost impossible to obtain except in the case of an official mission or by special favour on the part of the authorities. The Stalin Constitution is completely silent on this liberty of displacement Most of the individual liberties proclaimed by the new Constitu-

tion contain very broad formulae and are merely make beliefs 'Anything like real individual liberty is unknown in the USSR' (N De Basily *Russia under Soviet Rule*, p 183)

6 'The New Contitution' as stated in *Pravda* (June 18 1936) reflects one fact of exceptional importance that of the equality of rights of the intellectuals who are recognised as masters of the Soviet country, on entirely equal terms with the working classes and peasants '

IX

1 All citizens have an equal right of access to and use of, public roads wells and all other places of public resort

2 Every citizen shall have the right to keep and bear arms in accordance with regulations made in that behalf

3 Men and Women shall have equal rights as citizens (*Nehru Report*)

X.

1 No Law may be given retrospective effect

2 Domiciliary searches may not be made except in criminal cases

3 Neither landed nor movable property may in any case be confiscated

4 If the welfare of the State shall demand that any person shall surrender his movable or immovable property for the public use he shall receive full compensation from the Treasury (*Norway*)

XI

1. Congress shall make no law respecting an establishment of religion or prohibiting the free exercise thereof; or abridging the freedom of speech or of the press, or the right of the people peaceably to assemble, and to petition the Government for redress of grievances

3 No person shall be compelled in any criminal case to be a witness against himself nor be deprived of life, liberty, or property, without due process of law; nor shall private property be taken for public use without just compensation (*USA*).

APPENDIX V

GENERAL MINORITY RIGHTS

1 The nationals belonging to Minorities in the nation, whether based on religion or language have equal rights with other citizens in forming controlling and administering at their own expense charitable religious and social institutions schools and other educational establishments with the free use of their language and practice of their religion therein

2 Racial Minorities in the country have the right to establish autonomous institutions for the preservation and development of their national culture and to maintain special organizations for their welfare so far as is not incompatible with the interests of the State

3 In districts where the majority of the population belong to a Racial Minority the language used in the administration of local self governing authorities may be the language of that Racial Minority but every citizen has the right to use the language of the State in dealing with such authorities Local self governing bodies which use the language of a Racial Minority must use the national language in their communications with governmental institutions and with other local self governing bodies which do not make use of the language of the same Racial Minority

4 In towns and districts where a Minority speaks a language other than that of the Majority facilities shall be guaranteed within the limits laid down by general educational legislation to enable the children of such Minority to receive instruction in the official language. Instruction in the State language may at the same time be made obligatory.

5. In towns and districts where a considerable proportion of citizens belong to a Minority as regards race, religion or language, and where sums of public money are set aside for educational purposes in the State or Municipal Budgets or otherwise, a due share in the allocation and use of such sums shall be accorded to such Minorities, within the limits of the general regulations concerning public administration.

ARTICLE 80

6. "Nationals belonging to Minorities shall be treated on the same footing as other nationals as regards the exercise of agricultural, commercial or industrial callings or of any other calling. They shall only be subject to the provisions in force applied to other nationals."

ARTICLE 81

7. "Nationals belonging to Minorities shall have the right to establish, manage and control *at their own expense* charitable, religious, cultural and social institutions."

ARTICLE 75

8. "Legislative and administrative provisions may not establish any differential treatment of nationals belonging to a Minority. Similarly, they may not be interpreted or applied in a discriminatory manner to the detriment of such persons. The above principally concerns the supply of products subject to a centralised

system of exploitation such as articles of food coal, fuel paper used in the printing of newspaper etc., the distribution of means of transport the assignment of premises to persons companies or associations, the granting of official authorizations relating to transfers of real property and ownership measures relating to the distribution of land etc ' (From the German Polish Convention relating to Upper Silesia signed at Geneva on May 15 1922)

ARTICLE 77

9 All nationals shall be treated on a footing of equality as regards admission to public employments functions and honours including military ranks, and to public establishments and as regards the granting of degrees distinctions etc (Ib)"

ARTICLE 7

Differences of religion creed or confession shall not prejudice any national in matters relating to the enjoyment of civil or political rights, as for instance admission to public employments functions and honours or the exercise of professions and industries' (From the Treaty with Greece signed at Serves on August 10, 1920)

APPENDIX VI

SPECIAL MINORITY RIGHTS

I

INTRODUCTION

1. Minorities may be defined as groups of citizens who differ from the majority of the nationals of the State in regard to Race, Religion and Language

2. A Minority is entitled to full protection in regard to those of its interests in respect of which it is a Minority and differs from the rest of the citizens of the State. These interests will fall under one or other of the above three classes, Racial, Religious and Linguistic.

3. In regard to the administration and protection of these three classes of interests which constitute its cultural integrity and individuality, every Minority will have full powers of self-government, under a comprehensive scheme of cultural autonomy.

4. In regard to the interests which are not racial, religious or linguistic in their character such as economic, social or political, these are to be taken as the common interests of all the citizens and nationals of the State and cannot therefore be recognised as subjects calling for any special treatment or protection but as subjects of general administration

5. The elected Legislature is to have no jurisdiction in the sphere marked out for the cultural autonomy of a Community which will thus be placed outside the

rule of the Majority In this sphere the distinction between the Minority and the Majority will cease to be.

6 The League of Nations recognises only Linguistic Racial and Religious Minorities and rules out Minorities forming on other principles such as *Political* Minorities like the Liberals or Communists or *Social* Minorities like the non Brahmins Brahmins or Depressed classes or *Economic* Minorities like the Peasants or Industrial Workers The League s Scheme does not permit *Parties* to count as Minorities *Parties* may *differ and divide on live national* issues such as Economic Social Political or Administrative but the lines of such difference and division are not hard and fast ones or permanent in any sense The basis of the League Scheme of Minority Protection is that a Minority can differ from the rest of the citizens only in Language Race or Religion but cannot differ in any other matter There can be no differences of interest between citizens in matters of Law or Economic and Social Welfare matters affecting all citizens equally and as a whole and it is only these matters which are dealt with by the Legislature and Administration where accordingly there should be no place for any separate representation for any group of citizens through a separate electorate

Thus the theory of Minority Protection seems to be that such protection is not permissible for any artificial or accidental aspects or features which a Minority may acquire or assume in its career It must take its stand upon its native inherent fundamental features—its particular cultural characteristics These are respected so that a Minority community may develop along its own lines of evolution, and may, by its particular culture, make its own specific and appointed contribution to the general culture of mankind An article in the Polish Constitution "guarantees the full and free development of their national customs to Minorities" The Estonian Constitution lays down that 'Racial Minorities in the country have the right to establish autonomous institutions for the preservation and development of their national culture and to maintain special organizations for their welfare so far as is not incompatible with the interests of the State.'

There can be no case for the protection of a Minority in Legislature and Administration which cannot take cognisance of any differences between citizens, but are meant to function for the common interests of all Thus there is no case for such protective devices as (a) Separate Electorate, (b) Reserved Representation, or (c) Weighted Representation, for which there is not a single instance in any Western Constitution or Democracy with which each of these devices is incompatible

The advocates of these unheard-of devices for the protection of Minorities may be reminded of the noble words used by the late British Prime Minister J. Ramsay MacDonald in the Commons' debate on the first Indian Round Table Conference -

"If every Constituency is to be ear-marked as to community or interest, there will be no room left for the growth of what we consider to be purely political organisations which would comprehend all communities, all creeds all conditions of faith If India is going to develop a robust political life there must be room for national political parties based upon conceptions of India s interest, and not upon conceptions regarding the well being of any field that is smaller or less comprehensive than the whole of India. Then there is a modified proposal regarding that a proposal is made that there should not be Community Constituencies with a communal register, but that there should be a *common* register but that with a common register a certain percentage of representation should be guaranteed to certain communities It is the first proposal in a somewhat more attractive democratic form, but still essentially the same" The advocates of these proposals forget that "if you give one community weightage, you cannot create weightage out of nothing You have to take it from somebody else When they discover that, they become confused indeed, and find that they are up against a brick wall."

These words follow in the wake of the same constitutional tradition to which Edmund Burke gave expression in the following forceful words

' Parliament is not a Congress of Ambassadors from different and hostile interests which interests each must maintain as an agent and advocate against other agents and advocates but Parliament is a deliberative assembly of *one* Nation with *one* interest that of the whole where not local purposes not local prejudice ought to guide but the general good resulting from the general reason of the whole" (Bristol Speech)

A well-known judgment of the Privy Council delivered by Lord Shaw (Amalgamated Society of Railway Servants *vs.* Osborne, L.R. 1919, A.C.87), citing this classical passage, has held that the principles of community representation can find no place in the body of English Public Law.

But what is unconstitutional in England is made part of the Constitution in India against all principle, parallel, or precedent in democratic history and politics, theory and practice. The system leads to the absurdity that Mahatma Gandhi is not eligible for the vote of Maulana Abul Kalam Azad for election to the legislature, but is eligible for the vote of V. Savarkar, and Pandit Jawaharlal Nehru cannot vote for Mr. Rafi Ahmad Kidwai but can vote for Dr B. S. Moonje. The Constitution has indeed disenfranchised Indians as such They must divide as Hindus, Moslems, Christians and Parsis to acquire their franchise for purposes of election to what is devised as not an ordinary political parliament but a Parliament of Religions.

II

PROVISIONS FOR PROTECTION OF MINORITIES

A. LINGUISTIC

1. From the German-Polish Convention of May 15, 1922:

ARTICLE 105

"The needs of the Minorities as regards public elementary education shall be supplied by means of the following educational institutions

(a) Elementary *Schools* employing the Minority Language as the language of instruction i e Minority *Schools*

(b) Elementary *Classes* employing the Minority Language as the language of instruction, established in the elementary schools employing the official language i e Minority *Classes*

(c) Minority *Courses* including

(1) Teaching of the Minority language (*Minority Language Courses*)

(2) Religious teaching in the minority language (*Minority Religious Courses*)

ARTICLE 106 SEC 1

A Minority school shall be established on the application of a national supported by the persons legally responsible for the education of at least 40 children of *a linguistic minority provided these children are* nationals of the State and that they belong to the same school district that they are of the age at which education is compulsory and that their parents intend to send them to the said school

If at least 40 of these children belong to the same denomination or religion a Minority School of the denominational or religious character desired shall be established on application

' Should the establishment of a Minority School be inexpedient for special reasons, Minority classes should be formed."

ARTICLE 107

It requires at least 18 and 12 pupils for Minority Language Classes and Religious Courses respectively in the public elementary schools

ARTICLE 108

"Minority educational institutions may be closed unless the number of their pupils for three consecutive school years is less than the number required for their establishment

"Nevertheless the school may be closed at the end of one school-year if throughout that year the number of pupils has been lower than half the number required"

ARTICLES 117 AND 111

These lay down regulations on similar lines for "Secondary and Higher Schools"

As many as 300 pupils are required to claim separate Minority Schools for secondary and higher education, 30 pupils and 20 pupils respectively for the lower and higher classes for Minorities in the public schools, 25 pupils for separate Minority Language and 18 for Religious courses in the public schools

ARTICLE 122.

"Minority educational institutions (Secondary and Higher) may be closed if for three consecutive school years the number of their pupils is lower by at least 20 per cent. than the number required for their establishment

"If during one year the number of pupils is less than half the number required for its establishment, the educational institution may be closed at the end of the school year."

2. From the Lausanne Treaty with Turkey of July 24, 1923 ;

ARTICLE 41

"As regards public instruction, the Turkish Government will grant in those towns and districts, where a considerable proportion of non-Moslem nationals are resident, adequate facilities for ensuring that in the primary schools, the instruction shall be given to the children of such Turkish nationals through the medium of their own language. This provision will not prevent the Turkish Government from making the teaching of the Turkish language obligatory in the said schools."

"In towns and districts where there is a considerable proportion of Turkish nationals belonging to non-Moslem Minorities, these Minorities shall be assured an equitable share in the enjoyment and application of the sums which may be provided out of public funds under the State, Municipal or other budgets for educational, religious, or charitable purposes."

3. From the German-Polish Convention of May 15, 1922 :

ARTICLE 109

"The maintenance of Minority educational institutions shall be provided for according to the same principles as the maintenance of other State elementary schools."

ARTICLE 110.

"The Minority Schools shall receive a share, proportionate to the number of their pupils, of the funds allowed from the budgets of the school district for the ordinary maintenance of elementary schools, apart from general administration expenses and grants-in-aid.

ARTICLE 129

"If a private (Secondary or Higher) Minority school replaces a State Secondary or Higher School existing on the date of the transfer of sovereignty, it shall be entitled to a grant from public funds:

(a) Provided that the income of the school does not cover its necessary expenses. Income derived from school fees shall be estimated on the basis of at least the school fee in State schools of the same kind.

(b) And provided that the number of pupils who are nationals of the State amounts to either a total of 159, or an average of 30 per class in the four lower or 20 in the other classes.

ARTICLE 130

"Grants may only be made by communes or groups of communes if the commune or group of communes in whose area the private school is situated makes grants to State or private schools of the same grade, or if its expenditure on its schools of the same grade is not covered by the income of these schools.

"One of the bases for calculating these grants shall be the average amount of the grants or expenses disbursed per pupil.

"If the State, commune or group of communes declares its willingness and is actually prepared to admit a certain number of the pupils of the private school to a State Minority school or Minority classes in the same locality, the amount of the grant to be made to the private school shall be reduced by a sum proportionate to the number of pupils."

B. RACIAL

Racial Protection means that the peculiar manners and customs which mark out a community from other communities and establish its separate existence as a racial unit are to be recognized and respected by the State.

The provisions contained in the Constitutions indicated below will illustrate how the administrative arrangement regarding the racial protection of Minorities is to be worked :

ARTICLE 4

"The Turkish Government undertakes to take as regards non-Moslem Minorities, in so far as concerns their family law or personal status, measures permitting the settlement of these questions in accordance with the customs of those Minorities.

"These measures will be elaborated by special commissions composed of representatives of the Turkish Government, and of representatives of each of the Minorities concerned in equal number. In case of divergence, the Turkish Government and the Council of the League of Nations will appoint in agreement an umpire chosen from amongst European lawyers."

(From the Lausanne Treaty with Turkey of July 29, 1923).

ARTICLE 14

"Greece agrees to take all necessary measures in relation to Moslems to enable questions of family law and personal status to be regulated in accordance with Moslem usage" (From the Teraty of Sevres of August 10, 1920.)

ARTICLE 10

"The Serb-Croat-Slovene State agrees to grant to the Mussalmans in the matter of family law and personal status provisions suitable for regulating these matters in accordance with Mussalman usage" (From the Treaty with Serb-Croat-Slovene State of 10th September, 1929.)

C. RELIGIOUS

The religious protection of a community is taken for granted in every civilised State. It is not a problem affecting only the Minority. Religious protection is as much needed within a large majority community by its different sects. In fact, the larger a community the greater will be its internal differences in regard to religious views giving rise to different schools of doctrine and sects based on different practices calling for their protection.

The religious problem of Minorities in India sometimes takes a difficult form and baffles solution on the basis of mere theory or ideal. The problem of Music before Mosque appears to be of this character. Its solution may follow the lines laid down in the following provisions contained in the Turkish Constitution:

"All inhabitants of Turkey shall be entitled to the free exercise, whether in public, or in private, of any creed, religion, or belief, the observance of which shall not be incompatible with public order and good morals.

"Turkish nationals belonging to non-Muslim minorities shall enjoy the same treatment and security in law, and in fact, as other Turkish nationals.

"In particular, they shall have an equal right to establish, manage, and control at their own expense any charitable, religious, and social institutions, any schools and other establishments for instruction and education, with the right to use their own language and to exercise their own religion therein."

APPENDIX VII.

EXTRACT FROM THE VICEROY'S SPEECH AT CALCUTTA ON DECEMBER 17, 1942

"Geographically India, for practical purposes, is one. I would judge it to be as important as it ever was in the past, nay more important, that we should seek to conserve that unity in so far as it may be built up consistently with full justice for the rights and the legitimate claims of the minorities, whether those minorities be great or small. That that would be a desirable aim no one, gentlemen, can doubt who tests that proposition in terms of foreign policy, of tariff policy, of defence policy, of industrial development. Can India speak with the authority that she is entitled to claim ? Can she play her part effectively at international discussions, at discussions with the other parts of the Empire, if she is to speak with two voices? "